Fun Games for Soccer Training

Joseph A. Luxbacher, PhD
Head Soccer Coach
University of Pittsburgh

LEISURE PRESS

Champaign, Illinois

Library of Congress Cataloging-in-Publication Data

Luxbacher, Joseph A.
  Fun games for soccer training.

  1. Soccer—Training. 2. Soccer—Coaching. I. Title.
GV943.9.T7L89 1987   796.334'07   86-27198
ISBN 0-88011-283-2

Developmental Editor: Steve Houseworth; Copy Editor: Patrick
O'Hayer; Assistant Editor: Janet Beals; Production Director: Ernie Noa;
Assistant Production Director: Lezli Harris; Typesetter: Sandra Meier;
Text Design: Keith Blomberg; Text Layout: Denise Peters; Cover
Design: Michael Thomas; Cover Photo: James E. Corley; Illustrations
By: Mike McPhillips; Printed By: Versa Press

ISBN: 0-88011-283-2

Printed in the United States of America   10 9 8 7 6 5

Leisure Press
A division of Human Kinetics Publishers
Box 5076, Champaign, IL 61825-5076
1-800-747-4457

Canada: Human Kinetics Publishers, P.O. Box 2503, Windsor, ON
N8Y 4S2
1-800-465-7301 (in Canada only)

Europe: Human Kinetics Publishers (Europe) Ltd., P.O. Box IW14,
Leeds LS16 6TR, England
(0532) 781708

Australia: Human Kinetics Publishers, P.O. Box 80, Kingswood 5062,
South Australia
618-374-0433

New Zealand: Human Kinetics Publishers, P.O. Box 105-231,
Auckland 1
(09) 309-2259

Acknowledgments

This book would not have been possible without the help and cooperation of a great many people. Although the list is in no way complete, I would like to express my appreciation to the following:

Marianne Kennedy-Evans for her expertise in conceptualizing the illustrations.

Gene Klein for his assistance in preparing the Games for Goalkeeper Training.

Francis Luxbacher for his insight regarding the contents of this book.

Dorothy Zischkau for her help in preparing the manuscript.

Gail Ann Polkis for her assistance in proofreading the manuscript.

The many coaches and players who were willing to share thoughts and ideas.

For my mother and father, who always encouraged me to enjoy the game, for Kirsten Marie, and for the many coaches who unselfishly volunteer their time and efforts.

Contents

Foreword

I began playing soccer as a young boy. At that time, kicking a ball, running around a field, and playing with friends was just plain fun. Many of you are youth soccer coaches looking for a book that provides games and exercises you can use to teach and develop skills. Don't forget, however, that the best way to encourage players to work hard and to develop their skills is to make practices seem like just plain fun. In *Fun Games for Soccer Training*, Joe Luxbacher has achieved the balance between providing structured games for developing skills and making practices fun for everyone.

Two specific features impressed me while reviewing this book. First, coaches have 82 fully developed games that are applicable for developing all individual and most team playing skills. As a professional player who has developed through the American soccer system, I am aware of the practical problems of coaching young athletes in a sport that many of them did not play and learn as they did football, baseball, and basketball. Fortunately, soccer is an easy game to learn. Now, with *Fun Games for Soccer Training*, coaching soccer can be a bit easier for you as well. In fact, many of the games in this book can also be used with highly skilled soccer players. The second impressive feature is that players will benefit from games that are activity oriented and that stress playing under controlled situations, particularly competitive, game-like situations. Children love to challenge themselves, play keep-away, score goals, and have the opportunity to correct mistakes. The games in this book are designed to provide all of these aspects of soccer training. In particular, the coaching points provided with each game indicate the common errors that players make, essentials of the soccer skills used, and the right approach to take with young players to help them improve.

As a player who has reached a high level of expertise in soccer, I also understand and appreciate great soccer players. Great players come from years of hard work and countless hours of perfecting individual skills and team play. Great players, however, begin with young players who simply love to play soccer and, because of this, continue to develop skills as they mature. By making soccer training fun for all young people, Joe Luxbacher has written a book that can be used to develop great soccer players.

The 82 practice exercises compiled in *Fun Games for Soccer Training* are intended to aid in the development of the skills, fitness, and tactical understanding of the beginning and intermediate level soccer player. The player, however, is not the only beneficiary of the lessons to be learned from these exercises. Just as young players develop their skills and tactical awareness, so too must coaches add to their knowledge of the game. With the aid of this book coaches can learn along with their players and, most importantly, enjoy doing it. As a player who has honed his skills with many of these exercises, I can attest to the simple pleasures these games furnish. As a part-time coach, I can appreciate their effectiveness as teaching instruments. These exercises produce results because they combine learning and enjoyment.

Players will find the exercises enjoyable because each drill utilizes one or more balls. The use of several balls means more opportunities for players to touch the ball, which helps to enhance individual skills. Not only are the exercises more worthwhile from a learning point of view, they are more enjoyable for the player. A player's enjoyment of an exercise is directly related to the number of chances the player has to touch the ball. "Shadow Dribbling" is a good example of a drill in which players are constantly working to refine their skills while having fun.

Players will also find practices fun because the training exercises are competitive. In games such as "All Versus All" players have the opportunity to test their skills against each other. Additionally, many of the drills are fun simply because they offer a change from the routine of practice. "Crab Soccer" is an excellent substitute for push-ups or leg exercises because it is a fun game that includes the ball. Fitness exercises or fun games utilizing the ball are more effective than straight running because they force players to think and maintain control of the soccer ball while doing the running necessary for soccer fitness.

Coaches can enjoy practices more because they no longer need to spend their own valuable time designing drills for practice sessions. Coaches now can concentrate on coaching. To further develop coaching skills, the author has included coaching points. By observing these points, coaches can help their players while broadening their own knowledge of the game. Also, coaches will enjoy practices because these drills are easy to set up and execute. Soccer players want to play soccer. They do not want to spend valuable field time listening to a coach talk while attempting to execute difficult drills. These simple fun games are more effective than are difficult-to-understand drills.

Most important to coaches, however, is the value (utility) of these fun games. They teach the fundamentals and emphasize the skills necessary to become a complete player. In addition, they are extremely versatile. Each game can be made more difficult by adding defenders who reduce the time and space an opponent has to play the ball. At a recent training session my professional team played "Passing by the Numbers." The coach made the exercise difficult by varying the passing sequences and by introducing defenders, one by one, until the teams were even. Finally the exercise was made to simulate match conditions by going to goal only after a clean succession of passes. The exercise was fun and challenging even for skilled professionals. Whether the drill is shaped to test the novice or the professional, it is still fun and functional for players and coaches.

In closing I want to emphasize to coaches the importance of players having fun while learning soccer skills and being allowed to enjoy the experiences the game has to offer. This is particularly true with young players. Like many of you, when working with younger players I am often torn between teaching skills and playing games that emphasize the joys of the sport. This collection of soccer exercises solves this dilemma because it allows all players to have fun while they learn.

As coaches and players, our common goal should be to produce the best players we can, leading ultimately to the fielding of a team of native Americans who can compete equally with the rest of the world. As part of one of the first generations of native Americans to play and coach soccer, we also have an obligation to promote the game to a public often reluctant to accept soccer for what it is. We can achieve this by teaching eager young players what a great and fun game soccer is while helping them learn the skills to master it. *Fun Games for Soccer Training* is a vehicle by which we can reach our goal.

John O'Hara, Minnesota Strikers

Preface

Soccer provides a common language among peoples of diverse backgrounds and heritages, a bond that transcends geographical as well as ideological barriers. Known internationally as "football," soccer is the world's most popular game. Nearly every country in Europe, Asia, South America, and Africa lists soccer as its national sport. Soccer remains the only football-type competition played at the Olympic Games. Millions more people watch the World Cup, soccer's international championship, than our own NFL Super Bowl. It is truly the sport of the masses.

In recent years soccer's universal appeal has touched the hearts of millions of Americans. Among children and young adults it is our fastest growing team sport. Soccer's popularity does not rest on the fact that it is an easy game to play. In fact, soccer is probably the most demanding of all sports. Although one need not be any particular size or shape to play soccer, the game requires players to develop a high level of fitness, skill, and tactical awareness. Players do not acquire these essential characteristics by chance. The coach must assume responsibility for preparing his or her participants for the many challenges of soccer.

The tremendous increase in the number of soccer participants has created a pressing demand for qualified coaches. Many adults, either by choice or necessity, have entered the soccer coaching ranks. Although most exude unbridled enthusiasm and are motivated by good intentions, many of these individuals often have little or no experience. In order to be effective teachers they must acquire a basic understanding of the principles of learning and the philosophies of coaching.

No standard formula will ensure coaching success. Coaches, like players, are individuals. Thus many different coaching styles exist and have proven successful. What works for one might not be appropriate for another. Regardless of the methods employed, however, coaching philosophies should reflect one overriding theme—training should be fun! This all-important aspect of sport is often forgotten, in part due to the great emphasis placed upon winning as a measure of success. Practice sessions are typically viewed only as a means to an end. The result is a highly stressful training environment for players that is tedious and boring—in essence, a poor learning situation. Such an approach is wrong; practice does not have to be drudgery.

Coaches can incorporate a variety of fun game competitions into practice sessions, games that will nurture the technical and tactical development of players and create an enjoyable practice atmosphere. The key is to keep players active, involved, and interested. Children as well as adults respond more favorably if they are enthusiastic about what they are doing. This is not to imply that basic drills have no place in the practice regimen. However, the optimal learning environment should include a balance between typical soccer drills and the games described in the following chapters.

Training sessions must be organized to maximize the use of available time. Quality, not quantity, is the primary consideration. The games described in this book can be effectively used toward that aim. Each game accomplishes one or more of the following objectives: warm-up, skill training, tactical training, and fitness training. For example, a particular game designed to improve skills and develop fitness may involve passing skills coupled with off-the-ball running patterns. The games have been grouped into two general categories: Games for Field Player Training and Games for Goalkeeper Training.

The purpose of this book is to provide fellow coaches with a variety of fun games for use in their training sessions. Innovative coaches will use these games, or variations thereof, to provide players with an enjoyable learning experience and at the same time generate comradeship among teammates.

Joseph A. Luxbacher

SECTION I

Games for
Field Player Training

Field players must be physically and mentally prepared to perform the skills and tactics required for successful play. A sound fitness base is the cornerstone upon which performance is built.

Physical fitness for soccer is specific and consists of several key elements. Flexibility and agility involve one's range of motion and potential for executing precise skill movements. Endurance for general as well as specific muscle groups is essential to prevent diminished performance as players become fatigued in the later stages of a match. Speed is also an important component. Soccer-specific speed is a complex concept and involves much more than straight-out sprinting speed. Quickness over short distances is actually more important. This can be developed through exercises involving sudden changes of speed and direction while utilizing feinting movements with the ball. Finally, training for physical strength and power will prepare players to withstand the challenge of opponents vying for possession of the ball.

Fitness alone is not enough to guarantee success. Players must develop expertise in performing the various soccer skills. Basic techniques include passing, receiving, heading, dribbling, shooting, and shielding. Skill training should take place under game related pressures of limited time, restricted space, fatigue, and the determined efforts of an opponent.

Tactics involve organization and decision making individually and as a team. Individual tactics encompass the principles of attack and defense in a one-on-one (sometimes called man-to-man) situation. Small group tactics refer to situations involving three or more players (two on one, three on one, three on two, four on three, etc.). Team tactics deal with organizing players into systems of play.

The fun games described in the following sections are designed to promote the development of fitness, skill, and tactical ability in field players. Most involve two or perhaps all three aspects in the same exercise. Coaches may choose to emphasize one aspect more than the others depending on the objectives of a particular practice session.

GAME 1

Soccer Dodge Ball

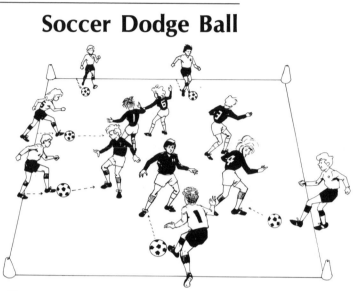

Objectives.

To improve passing accuracy, including hitting a moving target; to improve dribbling skills; to develop agility, mobility and general fitness.

Equipment.

Cones, small flags, shirts, or shoes to mark the playing area. At least one ball for every two players.

Organization.

Play with between 12 and 24 players, and divide them into two equal teams. Station one team, designated as Team 1, in a playing area 25 by 35 yards; they are without soccer balls. Members of the other team, designated as Team 2, each have a ball but must begin from outside the playing area.

Directions.

At your command, Team 2 players dribble into the area and try to pass the ball to hit players on the other team. Team 1 players can move to avoid being hit because if they are hit, they are eliminated from the game. All passes must hit players below the waist or they are not eliminated. After Team 1 is eliminated, the teams switch roles so that Team 1 passes to hit Team 2. The team that eliminates all opponents in the shortest amount of time wins. You can play this game several times or have the best two out of three games contests.

Coaching Points.

Emphasize passing accuracy rather than speed or power. Encourage players to dribble as close to their intended targets as possible before passing the ball.

GAME 2

Wide Support Game (3 on 1)

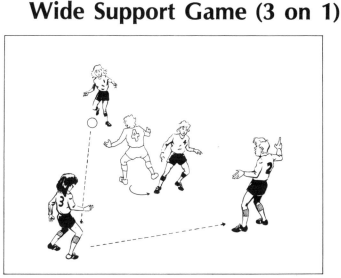

Objectives.

To develop proper support positioning by players away from the ball; to improve passing and receiving skills.

Equipment.

Cones, flags, shirts, or shoes to mark the playing area. One ball for each group of four players.

Organization.

Divide players into groups of four. Three players are attackers and one is a defender. Position each group in an area approximately 12 by 12 yards; the playing area may be reduced for highly skilled players.

Directions.

Games begin with the three attackers interpassing to maintain possession from the single defender. Attackers can score a goal by completing 10 consecutive passes. The passing sequence is broken if the defender wins the ball or if the ball leaves the playing area. The player who loses possession becomes the defender. Games continue for 10 to 20 minutes depending upon age and ability level of players.

Coaching Points.

Remind players that the primary objective of support positioning is to provide the player in possession of the ball with two short passing options. Emphasize that support players should position themselves at wide angles to the ball to provide clear passing lanes. Encourage players not to position themselves behind the defender and to readjust their position as the ball changes location. You can limit the number of touches that players are permitted before passing the ball to make the games more difficult. For example, attackers may be restricted to one- or two-touch passing.

GAME 3

Splitting the Defense (4 on 2)

Objectives.

To develop player movement away from the ball and to support positioning for attacks using passes that split the defense, also called penetrating or killer passes; to develop proper cover positioning of the support defender.

Equipment.

Cones, flags, shoes, or shirts to mark the playing grid. Colored scrimmage vests to differentiate attackers from defenders. One ball per group.

Organization.

Divide players into groups of six. Two players are defenders and four are attackers. Each group is positioned in an area about 12 by 24 yards; the size of the area may be reduced for highly skilled players.

Directions.

Games begin with the four attackers passing to maintain possession of the ball. Points can be scored by completing 10 consecutive passes for 1 point and by passing between the two defenders for 2 points. The passing sequence is broken when the defenders win possession of the ball or if the ball is played out of the area. The player who loses possession switches positions with one of the defenders. Play games for 20 to 25 minutes.

Coaching Points.

Encourage attackers to spread out, to attack with width and depth. Teammates should provide offensive support at wide angles to either side of the ball and should look to split the defense with killer passes. Remind players to adjust their support positioning as the ball changes location. Defenders should pressure the attackers to limit their passing options. The defender away from the ball, also called the *support* or *second defender*, must cover any passing lanes to prevent killer passes.

GAME 4

Passing by the Numbers

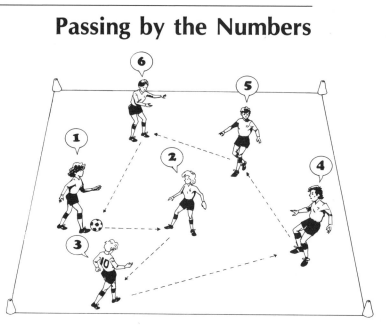

Objectives.

To improve passing and receiving skills under gamelike situations; to develop general endurance.

Equipment.

Cones, flags, shoes, or shirts to mark the playing area. One ball for every three or four players.

Organization.

Divide team into groups of 6 to 12. Each player calls out a number, beginning with 1 and continuing up to the number of players. Position players in an area of about 40 by 50 yards. If a regulation field is marked, play on one half of the field.

Directions.

The game begins with all players jogging within the field area. Those with a ball dribble, locate the teammate numbered directly above them, and pass to that person. The player with the highest number passes to Player 1 to complete the cycle. As soon as a player passes, he or she must be ready to receive a pass from the player numbered below him or her. Thus all players with or without the ball should continuously move throughout the exercise to pass or receive passes. Play for 10 to 15 minutes.

Coaching Points.

Emphasize that players receive the ball in a fluid manner. The ball should not be stopped completely; it should be received and controlled in the direction of the player's next movement. Encourage players to strive for accuracy and correct pace of passes.

You have the option of placing restrictions or conditions on the game in order to improve weaknesses of players. For instance, you could specify that players may pass only with the left foot or only use chip passes. Similarly, restrictions can be specified for the method used in receiving passes such as only with the outside of the foot or only with the inside of the foot.

GAME 5

Nutmeg Races

Objectives.

To improve dribbling ability in a confined area; to develop general endurance.

Equipment.

Cones, flags, shirts, or shoes to mark the playing area. At least one ball for every two players.

Organization.

Play with an unlimited number of players and divide them into two teams. Position players from one team, designated Team 1, an equal distance apart within an area approximately 15 by 15 yards; they do not have soccer balls and must remain stationary with feet spread apart. Players of the other team, designated Team 2, each have a ball and begin outside the playing area.

Directions.

The game consists of two 5-minute halves. On your command Team 2 players dribble into the area and pass the ball through the legs, or nutmeg, as many opponents as they can in the time allotted. Players may not nutmeg the same opponent twice in succession; they must continually move from one to another. Each player tallies how many successful nutmegs he or she accomplishes. Individual totals are combined for the team score at the conclusion of the first half of play.

For the second half of play members of Team 2 take positions in the area as stationary targets, and Team 1 attempts to total as many nutmegs as possible. Compare team scores at the end of time; the team with the most nutmegs wins.

Coaching Points.

Emphasize close control of the ball and fluid movement. Encourage players to keep their heads up as much as possible when dribbling to maintain good field vision.

GAME 6

All Versus All

Objectives.

To improve dribbling, shielding, and tackling skills; to develop general fitness.

Equipment.

Cones, flags, shirts, or shoes to mark the playing area. One ball for each player.

Organization.

Play with between 10 and 20 players. All players, each with a ball, are stationed within the designated playing area. The size of the area may vary depending upon the number of players; it should be crowded so that players practice dribbling and feinting skills while moving among teammates.

Directions.

All players dribble within the area while avoiding teammates. On your command all players attempt to steal another player's ball and kick it out of the area. Players may not leave their own ball when attempting to steal someone else's ball. Players are eliminated from the game if their ball is kicked out of the area. The game continues until only one player, the winner, remains in possession of his or her ball. You may repeat the game several times.

Coaching Points.

Encourage players to use deceptive dribbling movements and proper shielding technique to maintain possesion of the ball. Emphasize that the block tackle is the preferred method of tackling to steal an opponent's ball. Discourage use of the slide tackle since players should not, whenever possible, leave their feet in an attempt to win the ball.

GAME 7

Chase the Rabbit

Objectives.

To improve passing accuracy; to develop general endurance capacity.

Equipment.

Cones, flags, shirts, or shoes to mark the playing area. Colored scrimmage vests to distinguish the *rabbits* from other players. Four soccer balls; two for each team.

Organization.

Play with an unlimited number of players and divide them into two teams of equal numbers. Both teams take positions in the playing area of approximately 40 by 40 yards. Each team possesses two soccer balls; two players on each team are designated as rabbits and wear different colored shirts.

Directions.

The game begins with teammates passing among themselves while attempting to get into position to hit the opposing team's rabbits with a kicked ball. Hitting a rabbit below the waist counts for 1 point. Rabbits must confine their movement to within the restricted playing area. Keep tally of each team's point total. The first team to score 10 points wins the game. You may choose to adjust the winning point total depending upon the age and ability of your players.

Coaching Points.

Emphasize that interpassing should be purposeful—to quickly move the ball into position to score a point by hitting a rabbit. Remind players away from the ball to support the teammate in possession. Passing accuracy should be emphasized rather than power.

GAME 8

Crab Soccer

Objectives.

To develop strength and power in arms, chest, and legs.

Equipment.

Cones, flags, shirts, or shoes to mark the playing area. Small portable goals. Colored scrimmage vests to differentiate teams. One ball per game.

Organization.

Group players into equal teams of five or six. Each game is played on a 20 by 30 yard field area with a small goal, 2 to 4 yards wide, positioned on each end line. Each team defends a goal while attempting to score in the opponent's goal.

Directions.

Games begin with one team kicking off from the center of the field. Basic soccer rules are in effect with two exceptions: (a) goalkeepers are not used; (b) players must move up and down the field in a crab posture, a sitting position with the body elevated off the ground by arms and legs. One point is scored each time a team kicks the ball through the opponent's open goal. Play games for 10 minutes or a predetermined number of points.

Coaching Points.

Encourage players to keep their bodies elevated off the ground for the duration of the game. In addition to strength training, crab soccer provides an enjoyable warm-up exercise.

GAME 9

Shadow Dribbling

Objectives.

To improve dribbling skills by developing body feints and other deceptive movements; to improve general endurance.

Equipment.

Cones, flags, shirts, or shoes to mark the playing area. One ball for each player.

Organization.

Play with an unlimited number of players and divide them into groups of two. Position all groups in an area approximately 50 by 50 yards. If a regulation field is marked, play on one half of the field. Each player has a ball.

Directions.

The exercise begins with each pair of players dribbling in single file; one leads and the other closely follows. Leaders are free to move anywhere within the playing area; followers try to imitate, or shadow, the dribbling movements of the leader. At your command the players reverse roles and the leader becomes the follower. The game continues for 5 to 10 minutes with players constantly switching positions at your signal.

Coaching Points.

Encourage players to keep their heads up as much as possible while dribbling to be aware of the movements of their leader. Emphasize fluid, controlled movement with the ball.

GAME 10

Seek the Cone (1 on 1)

Objectives.

To achieve tactical training for the one-on-one situation; to improve dribbling, tackling, and shielding skills; to develop general endurance.

Equipment.

Cones, flags, shirts, or shoes to mark the playing area. One cone for use as the common goal in each game. One ball for every two players.

Organization.

Divide players into groups of two. Station each pair in a 15 by 15 yard playing field. Position a cone to represent a common goal in the center of the area. Designate one player as an attacker and award him or her possession of the ball; the other player defends to start the game.

Directions.

At your command the attacker attempts to dribble past the defender and score by passing and hitting the cone with the ball. If the defender steals the ball or the attacker misses the cone with a shot, roles change and the defender becomes the attacker. Games continue nonstop until you signal end of time. Award 1 point for each pass hitting the cone. The individual who scores the most points wins the competition. Play games for 2 minutes followed by a 30 to 60 second rest. Games may be repeated several times or as a round-robin tournament with winners from one game advancing to play winners from another game.

Coaching Points.

Encourage the attacker to use feinting movements and deception to unbalance the defender. The defending player must constantly be aware of the position of the ball in relation to the goal. He or she should strive to maintain correct defensive posture and good balance. Emphasize to all players that immediate transition from defense to attack and vice versa must occur upon change of possession.

GAME 11

Shooting Cones in the Safety Zones

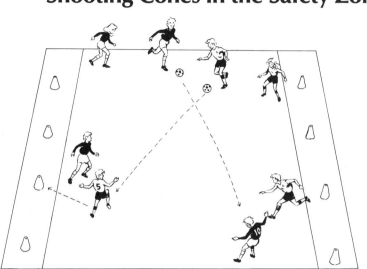

Objectives.

To improve shooting and passing accuracy; to develop combination interpassing among groups of players; to improve defensive marking ability; to develop general endurance.

Equipment.

Flags, shirts, or shoes to mark the playing area and safety zones. Ten small cones per game; two balls per game. Colored scrimmage vests to differentiate teams.

Organization.

Divide players into equal teams of four or five. Station two teams in a 30 by 50 yard area with a safety zone spanning the width of the field at each end. Place five cones an equal distance apart within each safety zone. Each team is given possession of a ball prior to the start of the game.

Directions.

Games begin as teams try to knock over the opponent's cones with a kicked ball while protecting their own cones. Players may not enter either safety zone; they attempt to hit opponent's cones by shooting or passing from outside of the zones. Any cones knocked over remain down to indicate the score at any point in the game. The team that first knocks over all of the opponent's cones wins the game.

The action is continuous. Loss of possession results when an opponent steals the ball, when the ball travels out of play, when a shot hits a cone, or when the ball passes through the safety zone. Otherwise, basic soccer rules apply.

Coaching Points.

Encourage combination passing coupled with creative dribbling and movement away from the ball to free teammates for a shot. Emphasize that defending players must position themselves to prevent the penetrating pass or shot that could hit a cone. Defenders must be aware of their position in relation to the ball and the cones.

GAME 12

Circle Tag

Objectives.

To improve mobility, agility, and general endurance.

Equipment.

Cones, flags, shirts, or shoes to mark the perimeter of the playing circle.

Organization.

Play with between 6 and 12 players. Divide them into pairs. Label each pair with a number. Begin with Number 1 and continue up through the number of pairs. Position players an equal distance apart around a circle with a diameter of approximately 20 yards. Partners stand directly across from one another on opposite sides of the circle.

Directions.

Begin the game by calling out one of the pairs, for example, "Number 3." Players with that number enter the circle. Designate one player as *it*; he or she chases and attempts to tag his or her partner. If he or she succeeds, roles change and the person tagged becomes the chaser. Players may not leave the circled area to avoid being tagged. Allow each pair 1 to 2 minutes of continuous tag before calling on another group.

Coaching Points.

Emphasize the use of quick changes of speed and direction to avoid being tagged. Encourage players to perform at maximum intensity for the entire time period to maximize fitness benefits.

GAME 13

Chain Tag

Objectives.

To improve mobility, agility, and general endurance.

Equipment.

Cones, flags, shirts, or shoes to mark the playing area.

Organization.

Play with an unlimited number of players. Designate two individuals as *it*; they begin outside of the playing area and serve as the initial link in their chains. Station all remaining players in the playing area of approximately 30 by 30 yards.

Directions.

At your command, the two players who are *it* enter the area and attempt to chase and tag free players. If successful, they link with the person tagged by holding hands to form a chain. As the game progresses and more players are tagged, the two chains increase in length. Chains may not split into numerous smaller chains while attempting to catch free players; only two chains are permitted at any one time. Continue until all players have been been tagged and are part of a chain. Repeat the exercise several times.

Coaching Points.

Encourage players to use body feints as well as sudden changes of speed and direction to avoid being tagged. Emphasize that the chains should work together to corner or trap free players. Depending upon the number of players involved, you have the option of increasing the number of chains permitted in the game. Because players are required to run continuously for several minutes, chain tag is an excellent warm-up exercise and also provides general endurance training.

GAME 14

Two on One (With Goalkeeper)

Objectives.

To develop tactical use of the give-and-go, or wall pass, to beat a single defender; to emphasize the individual defensive tactics used in an outnumbered situation; to develop an effective counterattack when moving from defense to attack.

Equipment.

Cones, flags, shirts, or shoes to mark the field area. Two small portable goals; if goals are not available cones or flags may be used to represent goals. One ball for every four players.

Organization.

Divide players into teams of two players each. Pair teams for competition. Teams play on a 10 by 25 yard field area; place a small goal, 4 yards wide, on the center of each end line. One team is given possession of the ball to start the game. The other team defends; one player is positioned as a defender and the other as a goalkeeper.

Directions.

At your command the team in possession attacks and tries to score while the defending team tries to win possession of the ball. Change of possession occurs either when the defender steals the ball or when the goalkeeper makes a save. The keeper may use his or her hands to save shots on goal. If the defender steals the ball, he or she must pass it back to the goalkeeper. Once the goalkeeper gains possession of the ball, from a backpass or by making a save, both players move forward to attack their opponent's goal. For the team losing possession, one player sprints back to cover the goal while the other positions as a defender. Teammates should alternate turns playing as the goalkeeper. Goals are scored by kicking the ball past the goalkeeper through the opponent's goal. The game is characterized by constant transition from attack to defense and vice versa. The team scored against is awarded possession after each goal. Play games for 15 to 20 minutes. The team scoring the most goals wins the competition.

Coaching Points.

Emphasize the advantage of a quick counterattack. Encourage attackers to use the give-and-go pass to beat the defender. The player with the ball should dribble in a direct route toward the goal to keep the defender committed before passing to his or her teammate. Defenders should position themselves to attempt to delay the opponent's attack and to force shots from narrow angles.

GAME 15

Speed Dribbling

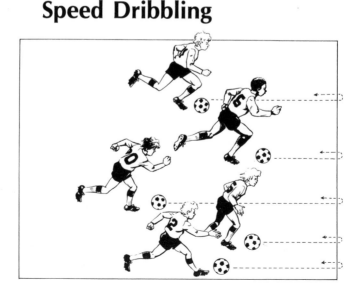

Objectives.

To improve dribbling speed in the open field; to develop general endurance.

Equipment.

Cones, flags, shirts, or shoes to mark the start and midway lines; if a regulation field is marked, use one sideline as the starting line and the opposite sideline as the midway line. Colored scrimmage vests to differentiate teams. One ball for each player.

Organization.

Play with an unlimited number of players. Divide them into two equal teams. All players line up with a ball 4 to 5 yards apart on the starting line. The midway line is marked parallel to the starting line at a distance of 50 to 60 yards.

Directions.

On your command all players dribble at maximum speed to the midway line, turn, and dribble back to the starting line. The team whose players all return their soccer balls to the starting line in the shortest amount of time scores 1 point. Repeat the race after a brief rest. The first team to win five races wins the competition.

Coaching Points.

Emphasize dribbling at maximum speed. Encourage players to push the ball ahead 2 to 3 yards and use long strides to sprint to it. Players should keep their heads up as much as possible while dribbling.

GAME 16

Wolves and Sheep

Objectives.

To improve dribbling speed and technique; to develop endurance and improve general fitness.

Equipment.

Cones, flags, shirts, or shoes to mark the playing area and safety zones. Colored scrimmage vests to differentiate teams. One ball for each player.

Organization.

Play with an unlimited number of players and divide them into two teams of equal numbers. Assign a name to each team, for example, Blues and Reds. Each player has a ball and is stationed within the 25 by 25 yard playing area. Designate two 5 by 5 yard safety zones in opposite corners of the area.

Directions.

At your command each player dribbles within the area—but not in the safety zones—and maintains close control of the ball. After about 1 minute of continuous dribbling, shout one of the team names, for example, "Blues!" At that signal, all players on the Blues try to dribble into either safety zone; the Reds leave their balls and attempt to tag Blue players before they can reach a safety zone. Players who chase are referred to as *wolves* while those trying to reach a safety zone are called *sheep*. Sheep may not be tagged once they reach either safety zone. Award a team 1 point for each sheep who reaches a safety zone. Repeat the exercise several times with teams alternating as wolves and sheep. The team totaling the most points wins the game.

Coaching Points.

Encourage sheep to use quick changes of speed and direction while dribbling to avoid being caught by the wolves. For advanced players, require wolves to dribble a ball while giving chase.

GAME 17

Throw, Receive, and Catch

Objectives.

To develop the ability to receive and control air balls; to develop correct support positioning by players away from the ball; to improve general endurance.

Equipment.

Cones, flags, shirts, or shoes to mark the playing area. Colored scrimmage vests to differentiate teams. One ball for each game.

Organization.

Play with 10 to 16 players and divide them into two equal teams. All players are stationed within the 30 by 40 yard playing area. One team is awarded possession of the ball to begin the game.

Directions.

At your command the game begins. The team with the ball tries to maintain possession by interpassing; the opposing team tries to steal the ball. Players interpass by throwing, not kicking, the ball to a teammate who must receive and control the ball with either the chest, thigh, instep, or head. After receiving with the appropriate body part, the player takes the ball in his or her hands and passes to another teammate. Players may not take more than five steps with the ball before passing. The defending team can steal the ball by intercepting passes or if an opposing player drops the ball to the ground. Defending players are not permitted to wrestle the ball away from an opponent. A goal is scored when a team completes 10 consecutive passes without dropping the ball or being intercepted. Play games for 15 to 20 minutes. The team scoring the most goals wins.

Coaching Points.

Emphasize the importance of player movement away from the ball. Support players must provide several passing options for the teammate in possession. Encourage players to cushion the ball as it is received by withdrawing the appropriate body part.

GAME 18

Headers Only

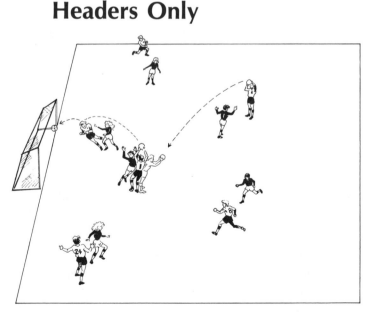

Objectives.

To develop tactical running patterns in support of the teammate with the ball; to improve the technique of scoring from headers; to develop general endurance.

Equipment.

Colored scrimmage vests to differentiate teams. One ball per game.

Organization.

Divide players into two equal teams of 6 to 14 players each. Play on a regulation soccer field with standard goals. Each team defends one goal and attempts to score in the opposite goal. Flip a coin to determine possession of the ball.

Directions.

At your signal the game begins with a kickoff from the center of the field. The team with the ball attempts to move into position to score by interpassing among teammates. Passing is accomplished by throwing and catching, not kicking, the ball. Once a player receives the ball, he or she may not take more than five steps before passing the ball to a teammate. Violation of this rule results in loss of possession to the opposing team. Goals are scored by tossing the ball to a teammate who heads it through the open goal. Goalkeepers are not designated for either team although all players may intercept passes with their hands. The defending team can gain possesssion of the ball by intercepting a pass, if an opponent drops the ball, or if the ball is played out-of-bounds by an opposing player. Defending players may not wrestle the ball from an opponent who has possession. Play games for 20 to 25 minutes. The team that scores the most goals wins the game.

Coaching Points.

Encourage players to move the ball upfield with short precise interpassing, not long tosses with a high risk of interception. Emphasize proper support of the player with the ball. When heading to score, players should attempt to head the ball on a downward plane toward the goal line. Defensively, stress one-on-one marking with each player assigned a specific opponent to cover.

GAME 19

Leapfrog Races

Objectives.

To develop upper body strength.

Equipment.

Cones, flags, shirts, or shoes to mark the start and finish lines.

Organization.

Divide players into groups of four. Groups take positions side by side on the starting line with players in each group organized in single file. The first player in each line leans forward at the waist and crouches with hands placed slightly above the knees. Mark the finish line 50 to 70 yards from the starting line.

Directions.

At your command the race begins. The second player in each line, Player 2, places his or her hands on the first player's upper back and vaults, or leapfrogs, forward and then also crouches in position. Player 3 leapfrogs over Players 1 and 2, Player 4 over Players 1, 2, and 3, and so on. The first team to get all players across the finish line wins the race. You can repeat the races several times or have a best of five games contest.

Coaching Points.

Encourage players to use their arms and chest muscles to vault upward and over teammates. Leapfrog races usually generate much laughter and enjoyment and also provide you with an excellent method of developing upper body strength and endurance in players.

GAME 20

Four Goal Game

Objectives.

To develop players' ability to change the point of attack toward the area of fewest defenders and greatest space; to improve general endurance.

Equipment.

Cones, flags, shirts, or shoes to mark the playing area. Colored scrimmage vests to differentiate teams. Four small portable goals; cones or flags may be used to represent goals. One ball per game.

Organization.

Divide players into equal sides of five to eight per team. Games are played on a 50 by 50 yard field area with a small goal 3 to 4 yards wide placed on the center of each sideline. Two teams play on a field; each team defends two goals and can score in two goals. Do not use goalkeepers. Flip a coin to determine possession of the ball to start the game.

Directions.

At your command the game begins with a kickoff from the center of the area. Teams score by shooting the ball through either of the opponent's goals below waist height. Regular soccer rules are in effect except that the offside law is waived. The defending team can gain possession by intercepting a pass, if the ball is played out-of-bounds, or after a score. The team scoring the most goals wins the game. Play games for 20 to 25 minutes.

Coaching Points.

Encourage attacking players to draw opponents out of position and then quickly redirect the play to exploit the open space. Defending players should constantly readjust their positions in response to movement of the ball. As a variation, you may play with two soccer balls at the same time.

GAME 21

Three Zone Game (3 on 4 on 3)

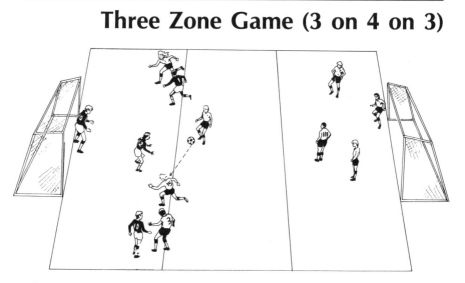

Objectives.

To improve attacking and defending ability in small group situations; to improve general fitness.

Equipment.

Cones, flags, shirts, or shoes to mark the field area. Two regulation size goals; if goals are not available use flags or cones to represent goalposts. One ball per game.

Organization.

Play with 10 field players and 2 goalkeepers. Divide the 40 by 60 yard field area into three equal 40 by 20 yard zones. Position one goal on each end line of the field. Station three players in one end zone, four players in the middle zone, and three players in the opposite end zone; a goalkeeper plays in each goal. Players stationed in the middle zone have possession of the ball to begin the game.

Directions.

On your command the players in the middle zone move forward into one of the end zones and attempt to score against three defending players and a goalkeeper. The defending players gain possession of the ball (a) by stealing the ball from an attacking player, (b) when a goal is scored or the goalkeeper makes a save, or (c) when a shot travels over the end line. After change of possession the three defending players move forward into the middle zone. One of the four original attackers joins them to assist their attack on the opposite goal; the other three original attackers remain behind in the end zone to play as defenders for the next shift. Players alternate as defenders and attackers, changing roles with each new attack on goal. Play games for 20 to 25 minutes.

Coaching Points.

Combination interpassing should be designed to free the extra attacker for a strike on goal. Emphasize that players should make a smooth transition from defense to attack when gaining possession of the ball. Encourage attacking players to move forward with speed and precision. In actual game situations any delay will allow defending players time to recover goalside of the ball to eliminate the one-player advantage.

GAME 22

Goal Scoring Derby

Objectives.

To improve shooting ability under game related pressures of restricted time and space, fatigue, and opposing players; to develop general fitness for field players and goalkeepers.

Equipment.

Cones, flags, shirts, or shoes to mark the playing area; if a regulation field is marked, play in one of the penalty areas. One regulation size goal per game. Six to eight balls per game.

Organization.

Play with seven players. Divide them into teams of three with the extra player serving as a neutral goalkeeper. Both teams are stationed in the 18 by 44 yard penalty area in front of the goal. Position yourself at the top of the penalty area with the supply of soccer balls.

Directions.

Begin the game by tossing a ball into the penalty area. Both teams vie for possession; the team that wins the ball attempts to score while the other defends. If a defending player steals the ball, his or her team attacks and tries to score. The goalkeeper attempts to save all shots. After a goal is scored or the keeper makes a save, or the ball is kicked out-of-bounds, toss another ball into the playing area. Continue the exercise until the supply of balls has been depleted or players are fatigued. The team scoring the most goals wins.

Coaching Points.

Encourage players to shoot at every opportunity. Emphasize the use of first-time shooting whenever possible.

GAME 23

Game With a Central Goal

Objectives.

To improve shooting skills; to develop defensive marking ability; to improve general fitness.

Equipment.

Cones, flags, shirts, or shoes to mark the playing area. Two flags to represent goalposts. Colored scrimmage vests to differentiate teams. One ball per game.

Organization.

Divide players into equal teams of three or four players each. Play games in an area approximately 40 by 40 yards; position two flagposts, each about four feet high, in the center of the playing area to form a goal 8 yards wide. Two teams are stationed in the field area with a neutral goalkeeper playing in the central goal.

Directions.

Begin the game by kicking a ball into the playing area. The team that wins possession attempts to score while the other team defends. Goals can be scored from either side of the central goal; the goalkeeper must readjust his or her position depending upon the location of the ball. A goal is scored when a shot passes through the goal below the height of the flagposts. A ball out-of-bounds is returned with a throw-in. The defending team switches to the attack after gaining possession of the ball. The goalkeeper is impartial and attempts to save all shots. After each save he or she throws or kicks the ball away from the goal but within the area. Both teams then compete for possession as play continues. Play games for 15 to 20 minutes. The team scoring the most goals wins the competition.

Coaching Points.

Emphasize creating and finishing scoring opportunities. Defensively, use a one-on-one marking scheme to reduce the time and space available to attacking players.

GAME 24

Circle Run

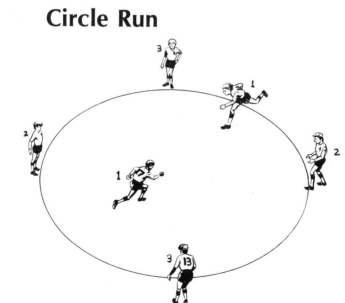

Objectives.

To develop general endurance.

Equipment.

Cones, flags, shirts, or shoes to mark the playing circle.

Organization.

Play with 6 to 12 players. Divide them into two equal teams. Pair each player with a partner who is on the opposing team. Label each pair, beginning with Number 1 and continuing up through the number of pairs. Partners line up directly across from one another on the perimeter of a circle with a diameter of 20 to 25 yards.

Directions.

Begin the game by shouting a number, for example "Number 2!" The two players labeled Number 2 change places by sprinting across the circle. The one who arrives first at his or her opponent's space is awarded 1 team point. Continue the game by calling on numbered pairs in random order. You may call two or three pairs at the same time. Play the game for 5 to 10 minutes. The team scoring the most points wins the contest.

Coaching Points.

As a variation you can increase the distance of the sprints. Require players to run across the circle and back to their original spot in order to maximize fitness benefits.

GAME 25

Circle Commands

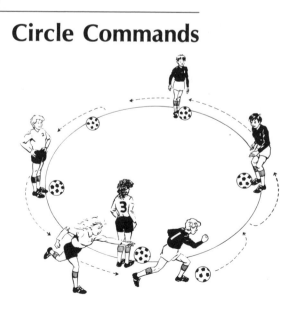

Objectives.

To improve dribbling speed and technique; to develop general endurance.

Equipment.

Cones, flags, shirts, or shoes to mark the perimeter of the playing circle. One ball for every two players.

Organization.

Play with 6 to 12 players. Divide them into two equal teams. Pair each player with a member of the opposing team. Label each pair, beginning with Number 1 and continuing through the number of pairs. Split pairs so that players are positioned directly across from one another on the perimeter of a circle with a diameter of 20 to 25 yards. One member of each pair has possession of a ball.

Directions.

Begin the game by calling a number, for example "Number 4!" Partners with that number sprint counterclockwise around the perimeter of the circle, one dribbling at top speed while the other pursues without a ball. The dribbler attempts to make one complete revolution of the circle before being tagged by his or her partner. If successful, he or she retains possession of the ball. If caught, his or her partner is awarded possession for the next round. After both players have returned to their original positions, continue the competition by calling on a different pair. Play games for 10 minutes.

Coaching Points.

You may adjust the circle size to accommodate the age and abilities of your players. The size should be such that the chaser has a reasonable chance of catching the dribbler. As a variation require the dribbler to make two complete revolutions of the circle before returning to his or her original spot.

GAME 26

Hot Potato (5 on 2)

Objectives.

To maintain possession through combination interpassing; to improve support positioning of players away from the ball; to emphasize the tactics used when defending in an outnumbered situation.

Equipment.

Cones, flags, shirts, or shoes to mark the playing area. Colored scrimmage vests to differentiate defenders from attackers. One ball per group of seven players.

Organization.

Divide players into groups of seven. Two players are defenders and five are attackers. Position each group in an area approximately 15 by 20 yards; the size of the area may vary depending upon the age and ability of players. The five attackers are stationed around the perimeter of the area while the two defenders are positioned in the center of the area.

Directions.

The game begins with the attackers passing to maintain possession of the ball. They are limited to one- and two-touch passing. The game is called *hot potato* because the ball is continually moving from one player to another. The attackers score 2 points if they complete 10 consecutive passes; defenders score 1 point each time they intercept a pass. If a defender steals the ball it is returned to the attacking team and the game continues. The attacking team is penalized 1 point if they kick the ball out of the area. Play games until either the defenders or the attackers total 10 points, and then select two different players as defenders. Repeat games until everyone has played as a defender for at least one game.

Coaching Points.

Emphasize player movement away from the ball to provide proper support positioning. Attackers should utilize the width and depth of the field area to create passing options for the player with possession. Encourage one defending player to pressure the attacker with the ball while the other positions himself or herself to provide support and to cover the passing lanes.

GAME 27

Soccer Keepaway

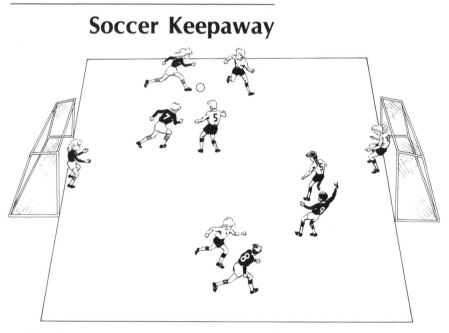

Objectives.

To maintain possession through combination interpassing and player movement away from the ball; to achieve tactical training for attacking and defending in small groups; to improve one-on-one marking ability; to develop general fitness.

Equipment.

Cones, flags, shirts, or shoes to mark the field area. Two portable minigoals required per game; if goals are not available, flagposts may be used to represent goals 5 to 6 yards wide. Colored scrimmage vests to differentiate teams. One ball per game.

Organization.

Organize teams of five players each, four field players and one goalkeeper. Two teams play on a field area 20 by 40 yards with a goal positioned on each end line. Each team defends a goal and attempts to score in the opponent's goal. Give one team possession of the ball.

Directions.

At your signal the game begins with a kickoff from midfield. Teams can score a goal either by kicking the ball through the opponent's goal below the height of the goalkeeper's shoulders or by completing 10 consecutive passes. Defending players can gain possession by intercepting passes or tackling the ball away from opponents. Except for the method of scoring, regular soccer rules are in effect. Play games for 20 minutes. The team scoring the most goals wins.

Coaching Points.

Encourage players to have patience in organizing the attack. At the same time, prepare them to look for and recognize the optimal time for a quick strike on goal. Emphasize maintaining possession until there is an opportunity to move forward and score. Use a one-on-one marking scheme to create high pressure situations for the player with the ball.

GAME 28

Feinting Cone to Cone

Objectives.

To develop feinting movements used to unbalance an opponent; to improve individual defensive marking techniques; to improve lateral movment and general mobility; to develop endurance.

Equipment.

Two cones per group used to represent goals. One ball for every two players.

Organization.

Play with an unlimited number of players. Divide them into groups of two. Each group marks off a straight line 10 yards long and places a cone at each end of the line. Each cone represents a goal. If a regulation field is marked, players can use a section of the boundary lines of the field. Partners stand on opposite sides of the line and face one another. One player has possession of a ball.

Directions.

At your command the game begins. While remaining on his or her side of the line, the player with the ball tries to beat the defending player laterally to either cone. Neither player may cross the line separating them. The defender may not steal the ball; he or she merely reacts to the movements of the dribbler. A goal is scored whenever the player with the ball dribbles to either cone before the defender can establish position there. Only the player with the ball can score goals. Play games for 2 equal periods of 60 to 90 seconds. Give the defender possession of the ball for the second period. The player who scores the most goals wins the competition. You may repeat the games several times or organize a round-robin tournament with winners advancing to a higher round.

Coaching Points.

Encourage the player with the ball to integrate deception and feinting movements with quick changes of speed and direction to un-balance the defender. The defending player should move laterally to front the ball while always maintaining a good defensive posture. In actual game situations, proper defensive positioning will prevent an opponent from playing a penetrating pass into space behind the defender. Remind all players of the basic rule of defense: Keep the play in front of you!

GAME 29

Heading Races—Front to Back

Objectives.
To improve heading technique.

Equipment.
One ball per team.

Organization.
Divide players into equal teams of four or five. Designate one player on each team as a server. Teams take positions side by side in single file. Each team faces its server who stands holding a ball 2 yards in front of the first player in line.

Directions.

The race begins on your signal and proceeds as follows. Servers toss a ball to the first player in their line who heads the ball back to the server and drops to his or her knees. The server then tosses to the second player in line who heads to the server and also kneels; server tosses to third person, fourth person, and so on. The server continues through the line from front to back until reaching the last player. At that point all other team members have headed and are kneeling. After the last player has headed the ball back to the server, the next to last in line stands up to receive a toss and head it to the server. The race continues, from back to front, until all team members are again standing and the server has control of the ball. The team that goes through its entire line of players in the least time, front to back to front, wins the race. The first team to win five races wins the series.

Coaching Points.

Emphasize the proper technique required to generate power and accuracy to the headed ball. Players should contact the ball on the flat surface of their forehead. To generate power they must arch their upper trunk and then snap forward as the ball arrives.

GAME 30

Triangular Heading Game

Objectives.

To improve the technique of scoring from headers.

Equipment.

Flags, shirts, or shoes to mark the playing area. Two flags per group to represent goalposts. One ball per group.

Organization.

Organize players into groups of three. Station each group in a 10 by 10 yard playing area and place a single goal 4 yards wide at one end of the area. One player is a goalkeeper, another stands to the side of the goal as a server, and the third stands 8 yards in front of the goal.

Directions.

The game begins as the server tosses a lofted ball into the area in front of the goal. The player positioned in front of the goal judges the flight of the ball, jumps, and tries to score from a header. The player in goal attempts to save. After the score or save, players rotate position. The player who headed moves into the goal, the goalkeeper becomes the server, and the server moves to the front of the goal. The game continues as players rotate positions after each attempt on goal. Goals are scored by heading the ball past the goalkeeper through the goal. Play games for 10 to 15 minutes. The player scoring the most goals wins the competition.

Coaching Points.

Encourage players to head the ball downward toward the corners of the goal. That type of shot creates the greatest difficulty for the goalkeeper.

GAME 31

Playing the Wall

Objectives.

To develop use of the wall pass to beat a defender; to improve support positioning of players away from the ball; to maintain possession through combination passing; to emphasize defensive responsibilities in an outnumbered situation.

Equipment.

Cones, flags, shirts, or shoes to mark the playing area. One ball per group.

Organization.

Divide players into groups of three and station each group in a 10 by 10 yard playing area. Two players are attackers and one is a defender. Attackers have possession of the ball.

Directions.

The game begins with the two attackers attempting to keep possession from the defender by interpassing, dribbling, and support movement away from the ball. The defender can gain possession by intercepting a pass or by tackling the ball from one of the attackers. Attackers can score points either by completing five consecutive passes for 1 point or by beating the defender with a wall pass for 2 points. The defender is awarded 2 points each time he or she wins possession of the ball. If the defender steals the ball, he or she returns it to the attackers and the game continues. Play games for five minutes. Whoever scores the most points, attackers or defender, wins the game. Repeat games with each player taking a turn as the defender.

Coaching Points.

Emphasize use of the wall pass to beat the defender. The attacker away from the ball should take a position at a wide angle of support with a clear view of his or her teammate. The player with the ball must make the defender commit himself or herself before initiating the wall pass.

GAME 32

Pressure Shooting

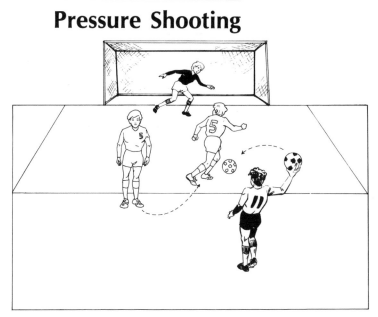

Objectives.

To develop shooting ability under gamelike conditions; to improve general fitness.

Equipment.

Cones, flags, shirts, or shoes to mark the playing area; if a regulation field is marked, use the penalty area. One regulation size goal. Six to eight balls per group.

Organization.

Organize players into groups of three. One player in each group is a shooter, one is a server, and one plays as the goalkeeper. The shooter stands approximately 22 to 25 yards from the end line with his or her back to the goal. The server stands 2 to 3 yards in front of the shooter with the supply of soccer balls. The goalkeeper is stationed in the goal.

Directions.

The exercise begins as the server tosses a ball behind the shooter who turns, sprints to the ball, and shoots to score. The shooter must strike the ball the first time it is touched; he or she may not control the ball before shooting. After each shot the shooter sprints back to his or her original position and the server tosses another ball into the area. Continue the exercise with the shooter alternating left and right footed shots until the supply of balls is depleted. The shooter scores 1 point for every shot on goal and 2 points for every goal scored. The goalkeeper tries to save all shots. Each player takes a turn as the shooter. The player who totals the most points wins the competition.

Coaching Points.

Emphasize first-time shooting. Encourage players to keep their shots low and on goal. In addition to improving shooting technique, this exercise is an excellent method of developing soccer-specific fitness.

GAME 33

Hunt the Fox

Objectives.

To improve the patterns of support movement of players away from the ball; to develop general endurance.

Equipment.

Cones, flags, shirts, or shoes to mark the playing area. Colored scrimmage vests to differentiate teams. Hats or other distinctive clothing to distinguish the fox from regular team members. Two balls per game.

Organization.

Divide players into two equal teams of 6 to 12 players and station them in a playing area approximately 40 by 50 yards. Designate one player on each team as a fox. Each team has possession of a ball to start the game.

Directions.

At your command the game begins. Teams can score points by hitting the opposing fox with a thrown ball. Passing is accomplished by throwing and catching the ball; kicking is not permitted. Players may take only five steps while in possession of the ball before passing to a teammate or throwing at the fox. Players can protect their fox by blocking or deflecting throws aimed at him or her. Change of possession occurs when (a) a player intercepts a pass thrown by a member of the other team, (b) a player makes an errant toss and the ball drops to the ground, or (c) a player takes too many steps while in possession of the ball. Two soccer balls are in play at all times. Score 1 point each time a team hits the opposing fox. Play games for 10 to 15 minutes. The team scoring the most points wins.

Coaching Points.

Emphasize player movement away from the ball to provide numerous passing options for the teammate with the ball. Proper support runs are necessary to move the ball into a position to hit the fox.

GAME 34

Dribble Freeze Tag

Objectives.

To improve dribbling skills; to develop general endurance.

Equipment.

Cones, flags, shirts, or shoes to mark the playing area. One ball per player except for the players who are *it*.

Organization.

Play with an unlimited number of players. Designate two players as *it* and position them without a ball outside the playing area. All remaining players with a ball are stationed within a field area about 20 by 30 yards in size.

Directions.

On your command all players begin dribbling in the field area. The two players who are *it* enter the area and attempt to tag the dribblers. Any dribbler who is tagged is considered frozen and must sit on his or her ball. Free dribblers can release the players who are frozen by tagging them. Play until all dribblers are frozen or for a period of 5 minutes, whichever comes first. Repeat games with two different players designated as *it*.

Coaching Points.

Encourage dribblers to use quick changes of speed and direction to elude chasers.

GAME 35

Soccer Golf

Objectives.

To improve accuracy in kicking a stationary ball over varying distances.

Equipment.

Six to 12 flags to represent holes. One ball for each player.

Organization.

Play with an unlimited number of players. Players can compete individually, one-on-one, or in teams of two or three. Position flag-posts to represent holes at various locations on an area 60 by 100 yards or larger.

Directions.

All players tee off with a placekick from a designated starting point. The ball must hit the flagpost to be considered in the hole. The basic rules of golf apply except that the ball is kicked rather than stroked with a club. Players move from one hole to the next until completing the entire course. The player or team completing the circuit with the fewest number of kicks wins the match.

Coaching Points.

Soccer golf is a suitable game to play the day before or the day after a match. The game provides a relaxing change of pace for players with little competitive pressure or physical exertion. As a variation, you may specify the type of pass to be used in kicking the ball or limit all kicks to the player's weakest foot. To incorporate fitness training into the game, require that players jog to retrieve the ball after each kick.

GAME 36

Circle Chip

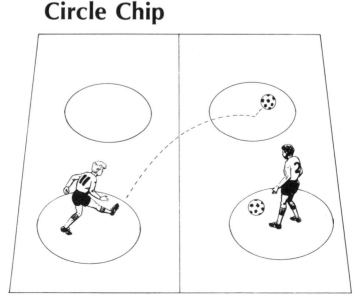

Objectives.

To develop accuracy for chipping passes.

Equipment.

Cones, flags, shirts, or shoes to mark the playing area. Four large circles distinctly marked with lime or other visible material. One ball for every two players.

Organization.

Pair players for competition. Mark two large circles in each half of the 20 by 40 yard playing area. Position each partner within a circle on opposite sides of the midline.

Directions.

At your command players attempt to chip a stationary ball from within a circle on their half of the field into a circle located on the opposite half of the area. Partners alternate chipping passes. Award 2 points for a chip pass that drops within a circle; award 1 point for a pass that bounces into a circle on one hop. Each player attempts 20 chip passes, 10 into each circle in the opposite half of the field. The player who totals the most points wins the competition. You can organize a round-robin tournament with the winner of each pair advancing to the next round.

Coaching Points.

Emphasize the importance of imparting sufficient loft to the chip pass. The ball should not be driven; rather, it should drop softly into the circled area. Encourage players to develop proficiency chipping balls with either foot.

GAME 37

Soccer Croquet

Objectives.

To improve passing accuracy.

Equipment.

Cones, flags, shirts, or shoes to mark the playing area. One ball for every two players.

Organization.

Organize players into pairs with one ball per group. Partners compete against one another. All pairs are stationed within a playing area approximately 60 by 100 yards; if a regulation field is marked, play on the entire field area.

Directions.

At your command the games begin. Players without a ball jog ahead of their partners. At a distance of between 10 and 20 yards they stop and spread their feet apart to form a tunnel. Players attempt to pass the ball through the tunnel for 1 point. After passing the ball, players jog ahead of their partners an equal distance and position themselves as tunnels. Players alternate attempts at passing and scoring. Play games for 10 minutes or a predetermined number of points. The partner who totals the greatest number of points wins the competition.

Coaching Points.

You may limit the distance the ball is kicked depending upon the type of pass emphasized. For instance, the inside-of-the-foot pass is most effective over distances of 5 to 15 yards while the instep-pass is more appropriate for distances greater than 20 yards.

GAME 38

The Jugglers

Objectives.
To improve ball control; to develop agility and flexibility.

Equipment.
Cones, flags, shirts, or shoes to mark the playing area. One ball for every three players.

Organization.
Organize players into groups of three. Station each group with a ball in a 10 by 10 yard area.

Directions.
At your signal group members begin to juggle the ball among themselves, using various body surfaces except the arms and hands to keep it airborne. Players may have only three individual touches of the ball before passing off to another group member. Assess 1 penalty point against a player whose ball drops to the ground or who leaves the playing area due to poor control. Any player total-

ing 10 penalty points is eliminated from the game. Play games until all players except one have been eliminated from each group. Reorganize groups with different players and repeat the games.

Coaching Points.

Encourage players to relax their body when controlling the ball. Beginners lack both confidence and ability and are often too rigid and tense. The key elements of successful ball control are confidence, concentration, and correct technique. All of those can be improved through ball-juggling exercises.

GAME 39

Breakaway and Score

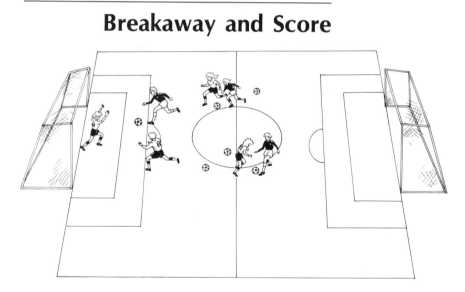

Objectives.

To improve dribbling speed; to develop general endurance.

Equipment.

Cones, flags, shirts, or shoes to mark the center circle. Colored scrimmage vests to differentiate teams. One ball for each player.

Organization.

Divide players into two equal teams. Label each team with a name, for example, Strikers and Sidekicks. Play games on a regulation field with goals. Teams defend one goal and attempt to score in the other.

One player on each team is goalkeeper; all remaining players with a ball are stationed in the center circle.

Directions.

The game begins with all players dribbling in the center circle. After approximately 30 seconds shout a team name, for instance, "Strikers!" At that signal all members of the Strikers dribble at top speed toward the Sidekicks' goal and attempt to shoot and score. The Sidekicks leave their balls and defend, trying to catch the Striker players and prevent them from scoring. The Strikers are awarded 1 point for every goal scored. Sidekick players are awarded 1 point for each ball they steal and dribble back to the center circle. If a defender merely kicks the ball out of play, neither team is awarded points. Repeat the exercise six to eight times. Randomly vary your commands so teams alternate between attacking and defending. The team that totals the most points wins the game.

Coaching Points.

Since the shortest distance between two points is a straight line, emphasize that players should dribble directly toward the goal. Encourage defending players to recover goalside of their opponent; they should not attempt to tackle the dribbling player from behind.

GAME 40

Piggyback Soccer

Objectives.

To develop leg strength and endurance.

Equipment.

Cones, flags, shirts, or shoes to mark the playing area. Colored scrimmage vests to differentiate teams. Two portable goals per game; flagposts may be used to represent small goals if portable goals are not available. One ball per game.

Organization.

Divide players into equal teams of 10 to 20. Play in a 20 by 40 yard area with a minigoal 4 yards wide positioned on each end line. Do not use goalkeepers. Each player pairs with a teammate of comparable size and weight. Award one team possession of the ball to begin the game.

Directions.

At your signal the game begins with a kickoff from the center of the field. Each team defends a goal and attempts to score in the opponent's goal. Regular soccer rules are in effect except that each player must carry his or her partner piggyback fashion during play. Partners change position every 60 to 90 seconds so that each shares the burden of carrying the other. Play games for 10 to 15 minutes. The team that scores the most goals wins the game.

Coaching Points.

Insist that partners be of comparable size and weight. To prevent injury, caution players to avoid physical contact with opponents—*play the ball, not the man*. This game may not be appropriate for very young players who lack sufficient strength and coordination. Use good judgment!

GAME 41

Zonal Dribbling

Objectives.
To develop dribbling skills; to improve tackling ability.

Equipment.
Cones, flags, shirts, or shoes to mark the playing area. One ball for every four players.

Organization.
Divide players into groups of four. Station each group in a 10 by 40 yard area sectioned into four zones of 10 by 10 yards. One player should be positioned in each zone; the player in Zone 1 has a soccer ball.

Directions.
At your command the player with the ball attempts to dribble the length of the area. To do so he or she must pass the players who defend in Zones 2, 3, and 4. Defenders are restricted to their assigned zone. If the dribbler beats the defender in a zone, he or she continues forward to take on the defender in the next zone. The dribbler scores one point for each defender beaten for a maximum possible score of 3 points. If a defender steals the ball, he or she returns it to the dribbler who advances to take on the defender in

the next zone. After moving through all of the zones, the dribbler remains in the last zone to play as a defender on the next shift while the other players each move forward one zone. The player originally stationed in Zone 2 moves into Zone 1 and becomes the dribbler. Play games for three to five complete rotations through the circuit. The player who totals the most points wins his or her group competition.

Coaching Points.

Instruct defending players to position themselves on the back line of the zone. This allows them to move forward and tackle once the dribbler enters their area. Encourage defenders to use the block tackle technique when attempting to win possession of the ball.

GAME 42

One-on-One With Support

Objectives.

To improve the individual defending and attacking tactics used in one-on-one situations; to improve general fitness.

Equipment.

Cones, flags, shirts, or shoes to mark the playing area. One ball for every four players.

Organization.

Divide players into groups of four; divide groups into teams of two players each. Station each group in a 10 by 20 yard area. One player from each team acts as a goal by standing with feet spread apart on their end line. Two players are positioned in the center of the field area for one-on-one competition. Give one of the central players possession of the ball.

Directions.

At your command the games begin. The player with the ball attempts to score by dribbling past the defender and passing the ball through the legs of the player positioned as a goal. If the defending player steals the ball, he or she tries to score in the opposing goal. Players positioned as goals may not stop the ball from rolling through their legs. Score 1 point for each ball passed through the opponent's goal. The players positioned as goals may not advance off the end line to assist in the attack although they can provide limited support for their teammates in the sense that central players may backpass to their goal and then move into open space to receive a return pass. Play games for 90 to 120 seconds. The team that scores the most goals wins. Repeat games six to eight times with players alternating between playing as a goal and as a field player.

Coaching Points.

Require that players positioned as goals have an extra ball in their possession. If the game ball is kicked out of the field area, the goal distributes the extra ball to his or her teammate to prevent any delay in the action.

GAME 43

Score by Dribbling Only

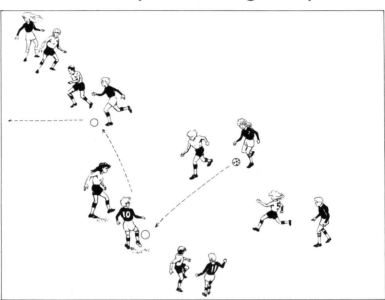

Objectives.

To improve dribbling ability; to develop one-on-one marking techniques; to improve general endurance.

Equipment.

Cones, flags, shirts, or shoes to mark the playing area. Colored scrimmage vests to differentiate teams. One ball per game.

Organization.

Play with between 12 and 16 players. Divide them into two equal teams. Station all players in a playing area approximately 40 by 60 yards with teams positioned on opposite halves of the field. A coin toss determines possession of the ball to begin the game.

Directions.

At your command the game begins with a kickoff from the center of the field. Regular soccer rules are in effect except that points are scored by dribbling the ball over the opponent's end line rather than by shooting. The entire length of the end line is considered to be the goal line. Players score 1 team point each time they dribble the ball over the opponent's end line. Play games for 20 to 30 minutes. The team that scores the most points wins the game.

Coaching Points.

Emphasize one-on-one defensive marking with each player assigned a specific opponent. Attackers should combine passing with proper support away from the ball to free teammates from their markers and allow them to dribble and score. Encourage attackers to take on defenders by dribbling in the attacking third of the field, the area near the opponent's goal line. Discourage excessive dribbling by players near their own goal line.

GAME 44

Too Few Balls, Too Many Players

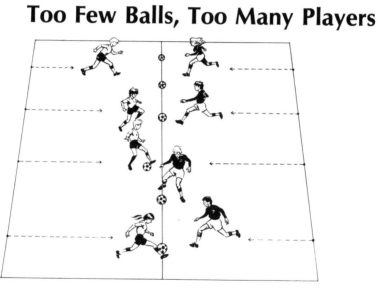

Objectives.

To improve dribbling speed; to improve individual defending techniques; to develop general endurance.

Equipment.

Cones, flags, shirts, or shoes to mark the playing area; the end lines and center line must be distinctly marked. Colored scrimmage vests to differentiate teams. Use two fewer balls than the total number of players.

Organization.

Play with between 8 and 16 players divided into two equal teams within an area approximately 25 by 50 yards. Bisect the field into 2 equal halves with a midline across the center. Position players along their respective end lines facing the center of the field. Place all of the soccer balls an equal distance apart along the center line.

Directions.

At your command players from both teams sprint to the center line, compete for possession of a ball, and attempt to dribble it over their own end line. Score 1 point for each ball returned over an end line. A ball must be dribbled under control, not kicked, over the end line to score a point. The two players not winning possession of a ball try to prevent opponents from scoring by stealing their soccer balls and kicking them out of the playing area. Repeat the exercise 10 times. The team that totals the most points wins the competition.

Coaching Points.

Encourage players without a ball to recover goalside of their opponents to a position where they can block tackle and win possession of a ball. Discourage use of slide tackles.

GAME 45

Slalom Dribbling Races

Objectives.

To improve dribbling speed and control; to develop general endurance.

Equipment.

Cones, flags, shirts, or shoes to construct the slalom courses. One ball per team.

Organization.

Divide players into equal teams of four or five players. Each team lines up in single file directly in front of a slalom course consisting of six to eight markers positioned in a straight line. Allow 3 yards distance between markers. The first player in each line has a ball.

Directions.

On your signal the race begins. The first players in each line dribble through the slalom course from front to back to front and exchange the ball with the next player in their line. All players in turn dribble through the course by weaving in and out of the markers. Award 10 points to the team whose players complete the slalom course in the least time, award the second place team 8 points, award third place 6 points, and so on. Players are penalized 1 point for each marker bypassed or knocked over during the race. Point totals are determined by subtracting the total number of penalty points assessed against team members from points awarded for the team's order of finish in the race. Repeat the races several times. The first team to score a total of 50 points wins.

Coaching Points.

Emphasize that speed as well as control are important aspects of dribbling ability. Encourage players to maintain close control of the ball as they weave through the slalom course.

GAME 46

Pressure Heading

Objectives.

To develop proper technique and timing for the jump header. To develop leg strength and endurance.

Equipment.

Cones, flags, shirts, or shoes to mark the playing area. Two balls for each group of three players.

Organization.

Divide players into groups of three. Place each group in a straight line within a rectangular playing area approximately 4 by 10 yards. The end players in line function as servers and face the middle player from a distance of 5 yards. Each server holds a ball.

Directions.

At your command the game begins as one of the servers tosses a lofted pass toward the middle player who returns the ball by jumping and heading. The middle player then turns to head a ball tossed by the other server. Continue the exercise with the middle player alternating jump headers to one server and then the other. Score 1 point for each ball successfully headed back to a server. Deduct 1 point for each inaccurate return to the server. The player heads for 40 seconds and then changes places with one of the servers. Repeat the exercise so each player gets equal time heading the ball. The player scoring the most points during his or her bout of heading wins the competition.

Coaching Points.

Correct technique and proper timing are essential elements for successful heading. Encourage players to jump up vertically, to arch their upper trunk backwards, and then to snap forward to meet the ball. They should contact the ball on the flat surface of the forehead. Limit the period of heading to 15 to 20 seconds for younger players.

GAME 47

Team Tennis

Objectives.

To improve players' ability to pass and receive lofted and bouncing balls.

Equipment.

Cones, flags, shirts, or shoes to mark the playing area. One tennis net or a rope stretched between two posts. One ball per game.

Organization.

Divide players into equal teams of four or five. Play games in a 20 by 50 yard area; divide the court in half with a net or rope approximately 3 feet high stretched across its center. If available, play on a regulation tennis court. Station one team on each side of the net. Flip a coin to determine which team serves first.

Directions.

The game begins as the server chips a stationary ball from behind his or her end line. The ball must travel over the net and land within the opponent's court to constitute a good serve. The receiving team may allow the ball to bounce only once before returning it by kicking or heading. Players are not required to let the ball bounce; they may use a first-time volley to return the ball. Teammates may also interpass in the air before returning the ball over the net into the opposite court. A fault occurs when (a) the serve fails to clear the net, (b) the serve or return lands out-of-bounds, (c) the ball is allowed to bounce more than once on a side, or (d) a player uses his or her arms or hands to pass or control the ball. Only the serving team can score points. Award 1 point to the serving team for each fault committed by the receiving team. If the serving team commits a fault they lose serve to the opposing team. The first team to score 21 points wins the game. Play best of three games series.

Coaching Points.

Encourage players to return the serve with first-time volleys whenever possible. Emphasize the importance of verbal communication among teammates. Teamwork as well as individual skills are required to successfully play soccer tennis.

GAME 48

Soccer Marbles

Objectives.

To improve passing accuracy; to improve dribbling and shielding skills; to develop general endurance.

Equipment.

Cones, flags, shirts, or shoes to mark the playing area. One ball for each player.

Organization.

Divide players into groups of three. Each group plays in an area approximately 20 by 30 yards. All players are positioned with a ball on one end line of the playing area. Designate one player as *it*.

Directions.

At your command the game begins. The player who is *it* dribbles within the area while the other players follow and attempt to contact the dribbler's ball with their own. Each hit counts 1 point. Players take turns being *it* for a period of 2 minutes each. The individual whose ball is hit the fewest times wins the game. You may repeat the series several times.

Coaching Points.

Encourage the player who is *it* to use quick changes of speed and direction to prevent other players from hitting his or her ball. The players who are trying to hit the dribbler's ball should move as close as possible before attempting to pass.

GAME 49

Chip and Defend

Objectives.

To improve players' ability to make chip passes; to improve the skills used for receiving lofted passes; to emphasize the defensive tactics used in an outnumbered situation.

Equipment.

Cones, flags, shirts, or shoes to mark the playing area. One ball for every three players.

Organization.

Divide players into groups of three and station each group in a 10 by 30 yard area. Position one player with a ball on an end line of the playing area. Station two players as attackers at the opposite end of the area.

Directions.

The game begins as the player with the ball chips a lofted pass to the two players stationed at the opposite end of the field area. After kicking the ball the server moves forward and becomes a defender. The attackers control the ball and advance to take on the server-defender in a two-on-one situation. The server-defender can score 1 point by accurately chipping the ball so the attackers can receive it directly out of the air or by stealing the ball from the attackers. The attackers score by taking on and beating the defender to the end line for 1 point. They must have the ball under control as they reach the end line to be awarded 1 point. Play games to 10 points; players switch positions after each game. Repeat the game three times so each player gets a turn as the server-defender.

Coaching Points.

Stress sufficient loft and accuracy for chip passes. Encourage the attacker dribbling the ball to pass only after the defender has committed himself or herself. Emphasize use of the give-and-go pass to beat the defender.

GAME 50

Throw It Long

Objectives.

To improve distance on the throw-in.

Equipment.

Cones, flags, shirts, or shoes to mark the playing area and midline. If a regulation field is marked, play on entire area. One ball for every two players.

Organization.

Divide an unlimited number of players into groups of two. Partners take positions an equal distance from the midline on opposite halves of a regulation size field. One player in each pair is given possession of a ball.

Directions.

At your command the game begins as players with a ball try to throw it as far as possible using the proper throw-in motion. Their partners catch the ball out of the air and return it by throwing from the spot where they received it. Partners alternate throwing the ball back and forth to one another. The players who eventually force their partners backwards over the goal line due to the greater distance of their throws win the contest. Set a time limit of 10 minutes per game.

Coaching Points.

The correct throw-in motion begins from behind the head with both hands positioned behind the ball. At the moment the ball is released, both feet must be in contact with the ground. Encourage players to arch their upper body and snap forward to generate maximum distance on their throws. You can organize a round-robin tournament with winners paired against winners until a grand champion is crowned.

GAME 51

Attacking With Reduced Numbers

Objectives.

To develop passing combinations; to improve shooting skills under gamelike conditions; to develop general endurance.

Equipment.

Cones, flags, shirts, or shoes to mark the playing area. One regulation size goal. Colored scrimmage vests to differentiate teams. One ball per game.

Organization.

Divide players into equal teams of two or three. Station three teams within a 40 by 45 yard playing area; if a regulation field is marked, play on one half of the field. Position a goal on one end line. A neutral goalkeeper plays in goal and has possession of the ball to start the game.

Directions.

At your signal the game begins with the goalkeeper punting the ball. All three teams compete for possession. The team that wins the ball tries to score while the other two teams defend. Goals can be scored from any distance using either the feet or the head. If a defending player steals the ball his or her team goes on the attack and tries to score. The neutral goalkeeper attempts to save all shots. After a goal is scored or the ball goes out of play or the goalkeeper makes a save, play is resumed with the goalkeeper punting or throwing the ball into the field area. Teams again compete for possession and try to score. Play games for 20 minutes. The team that scores the most goals wins the contest.

Coaching Points.

Encourage players to shoot at every opportunity. Because its players are outnumbered when attacking four defenders, the team with possession of the ball should attempt to isolate and beat the defending players using one- and two-touch passing combined with creative dribbling.

GAME 52

Diving Headers Game

Objectives.

To develop the ability to score from dive headers.

Equipment.

Cones, flags, shirts, or shoes to mark the playing area. One regulation goal. Ten balls.

Organization.

Divide players into two equal teams. Designate two neutral servers and a neutral goalkeeper. Teams line up in single file facing the goal at a distance of approximately 20 yards. If a regulation field is marked, use the penalty area as the playing field and have teams line up at the top of the area. Station a server 6 yards to each side of the goal with a supply of balls.

Directions.

At your command the game begins. The servers alternate tossing lofted balls into the goal area. Players from each team in turn run forward and attempt to score from a diving header. Each goal scored counts 2 team points and a ball headed on goal that the goalkeeper saves counts 1 point. Any shot that misses the goal counts zero points. Play games for 10 minutes or a predetermined number of points. The team that scores the most points wins the game.

Coaching Points.

Accurate tosses by the servers are needed for players to benefit from this exercise. Require that players master the correct technique of dive heading before attempting the skill in competition. One's arms and hands should be used to cushion the impact of the body with the ground. Dive headers may not be appropriate for very young players who lack adequate strength and coordination. Use good judgment!

GAME 53

Double Zone Soccer

Objectives.

To develop defending and attacking tactics used in a three-on-two situation; to improve general endurance.

Equipment.

Cones, flags, shirts, or shoes to mark the playing area. Colored scrimmage vests to differentiate teams. Two portable goals per game or use flags or cones to serve as goalposts. One ball per game.

Organization.

Divide players into two equal teams of five. Play games on a field approximately 25 by 50 yards with a midline bisecting the area into two equal zones. Position a small goal about 3 yards wide on each end line. Three players are attackers and two are defenders for each team; goalkeepers are not used. The three attackers take positions in the opposing team's half of the field while the two defenders are stationed in their own half, thus creating a three-on-two situation in each zone. Flip a coin to determine possession of the ball to begin the game.

Directions.

At your command the game begins. Each team defends a goal with two defenders and tries to score in the opponent's goal with three attackers. Players are restricted to movement within their assigned zone. If a defender steals the ball he or she initiates a counterattack by passing to a teammate in the opposite zone. After a goal the team scored against is awarded possession of the ball. Regular soccer rules are in effect; any infringement of the rules results in loss of possession. Play games for 20 to 25 minutes. The team that scores the most goals wins the game.

Coaching Points.

Encourage the defending players to work in tandem. While one defender pressures the attacker with the ball, the second defender provides cover to prevent a pass that penetrates the defense. Attacking players should use combination passing and movement away from the ball to free the extra attacker for a strike on goal.

GAME 54

Long Distance Shooting Game

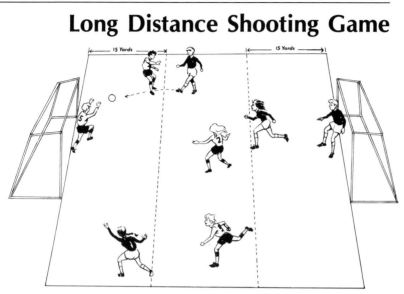

Objectives.

To develop power and accuracy for shooting from outside the penalty area; to develop general endurance.

Equipment.

Cones, flags, shirts, or shoes to mark the playing area. Colored scrimmage vests to differentiate teams. Portable regulation size goals. If goals are not available, flags or cones may be used to represent goals. One ball per game.

Organization.

Divide players into teams of four; three field players and one goalkeeper per team. Station teams in a 40 by 60 yard area with a goal positioned on each end line. Flip a coin to determine possession of the ball to begin the game.

Directions.

At your command the game begins with a kickoff from the center of the field. Teams attempt to score by shooting the ball through the opponent's goal. All shots must be taken from a distance of 15 yards or greater. The attacking team scores 2 points for each goal scored and 1 point for each shot on goal that is saved by the goalkeeper. Shots that miss the goal count zero points. Except for the scoring system, regular soccer rules are in effect. Play games for 15 to 20 minutes. The team that scores the most points wins the game.

Coaching Points.

Encourage players to shoot at every opportunity. Although all of the basic soccer skills may be used during the games, emphasize shooting with power and accuracy.

GAME 55

Monkey in the Middle

Objectives.

To improve chip pass technique.

Equipment.

Cones, flags, shirts, or shoes to mark the playing area. One ball for every three players.

Organization.

Divide players into groups of three. Station each group in a 10 by 30 yard area divided into three consecutive 10 by 10 yard zones. Position one player in each zone.

Directions.

At your command the game begins as the players stationed in the end zones attempt to chip the ball back and forth over the player in the middle zone. Players are limited to only two touches of the ball; the first touch is to control and the second touch is to chip the ball. Players in the end zones score each time they chip the ball over the player in the middle zone. The ball must travel from one end zone into the other end zone without touching the ground to count 1 point. Players are penalized 1 point if they need more than two touches to return the ball, if their pass lands out of the playing area, or if their pass doesn't clear the center zone. The player in the middle zone scores 1 point each time he or she intercepts a chip pass. Play games for a total of 15 points. Repeat games with players rotating to a different zone.

Coaching Points.

Instruct players to use a short, powerful motion of the kicking leg when chipping the ball. The player in the middle zone should constantly adjust his or her position to front the player who is kicking the ball to be able to intercept any low chip.

GAME 56

Goal Kick and Recover Goalside

Objectives.

To improve goal kick distance and accuracy; to develop general endurance.

Equipment.

Cones, flags, shirts, or shoes to mark the playing area. Two regulation size goals. If goals are not available, flags or cones may be used to represent goalposts. One ball per game.

Organization.

Play with six players. Divide them into teams of three. Designate one team as the attacking team, the other as defenders. Play on an area approximately 50 by 100 yards divided in half by a line drawn across the center of the field; if a regulation field is marked, play on the entire area. Position a goal on each end line. Station the three attacking players along the midline; two players from the opposing team position themselves to defend a goal. The third defender is in the opposite goal area with the ball. Do not use goalkeepers.

Directions.

At your command the defender with the ball serves a goal kick to the players stationed on the midline. The attackers control the ball and try to score against the two players defending the opposite goal. The player who served the goal kick sprints the length of the field to aid his or her teammates in defense. However, the server may not leave the goal area until the opposing team has possession of the ball at the midline. All shots must be taken from a distance of 18 yards or less because there are no goalkeepers. After a score or when the defense gains possession of the ball, play is restarted with a goal kick. Teams alternate turns playing as defenders and attackers. Play games for 15 to 20 minutes. The team scoring the most goals wins the game.

Coaching Points.

Encourage the attacking team to avoid any delay in taking on the two defenders. The numerical advantage of three attackers versus two defenders will not last long because the third defender will recover goalside of the attackers if given sufficient time.

GAME 57

Crabs and Fish

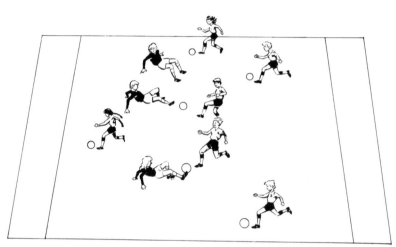

Objectives.

To improve dribbling skills; to develop upper body strength in the arms and chest; to develop general endurance.

Equipment.

Cones, flags, shirts, or shoes to mark the playing area. Approximately one ball for each player.

Organization.

Play with an unlimited number of players. Mark a rectangular playing area 20 by 30 yards with a safety zone 3 yards deep extending the width of the area at each end. Designate three players as *crabs* and station them without a ball in the center of the area. The crabs assume a sitting position with body weight supported by their arms and legs. Station all remaining players with a ball as *fish* in one of the safety zones.

Directions.

On your command the fish attempt to dribble the length of the area from one safety zone to the other. The crabs try to steal the balls from the fish and kick them out of the playing area. Crabs may not use their hands to play the ball. Fish become crabs if they lose possession of the ball or dribble out of the playing area. Fish who successfully dribble from one safety zone to the other zone remain there until the crabs adjust their positions to face the fish. At your signal the surviving fish attempt to dribble back to the other safety zone. The fish continue dribbling from one safety zone to the other until all have been caught. Repeat the games until three fish remain; they are designated crabs to begin the next game.

Coaching Points.

Fish may not chip the ball over the crabs when attempting to go from one safety zone to the other. The ball must be dribbled on the ground between the crabs.

GAME 58

Immediate Attack—Blitzkrieg

Objectives.

To develop tactics used for attacking with a numerical advantage of five players versus three; to improve the transition from defense to attack after gaining possession of the ball; to improve general endurance.

Equipment.

Cones, flags, shirts, or shoes to mark the playing area. Colored scrimmage vests to differentiate teams and to distinguish the neutral players from either team. Two portable goals about four yards wide; if goals are not available, use flags or cones to represent goalposts. One ball per game.

Organization.

Divide players into groups of eight. Within each group form two teams of three and designate two neutral players. Play games on a 20 by 40 yard field with a small goal positioned on each end line. Do not use goalkeepers. Flip a coin to determine possession of the ball to start the game.

Directions.

At your command the game begins with a kickoff from the center of the area. Each team defends one goal and attempts to score in the opponent's goal. The two neutrals play with the team in possession of the ball and do not defend for either team. If a defending player steals the ball, his or her first pass must be to one of the neutrals. The team then attacks five-on-three. Otherwise, regular soccer rules are in effect. Play games for 15 to 20 minutes. The team that scores the most goals wins the game.

Coaching Points.

Emphasize quick transition from defense to attack upon winning possession of the ball. The attacking team should use the width and depth of the field to spread defenders and free the extra attackers for a strike on goal.

GAME 59

Six Versus Four

Objectives.

To develop the team tactics used in attack and defense.

Equipment.

Cones, flags, shirts, or shoes to mark the playing area. Colored scrimmage vests to differentiate attackers from defenders. One regulation size goal and two minigoals 3 yards wide; if portable goals are not available, use cones or flags to represent goalposts. One ball per game.

Organization.

Divide players into groups of 11. Six players are attackers, four are defenders, and one plays as a goalkeeper in the regulation size goal. Station players in a 50 by 60 yard area with the regulation size goal on one end line and two minigoals positioned 20 yards apart on the other end line. If a regulation field is marked, play on one half of the field. Do not play goalkeepers in the small goals. Give the six attackers possession of the ball to begin the game.

Directions.

At your command the game begins. The attacking players attempt to score in the regulation goal against four defenders and a goalkeeper. Attackers can score by kicking the ball past the goalkeeper through the goal for 2 points or by taking a shot that the goalkeeper saves for 1 point. If the attackers score a goal they retain possession of the ball but must restart the attack from their end line. Defenders can gain possession of the ball by receiving a pass from the goalkeeper after a save or by stealing the ball from the attackers. Defenders score 1 point each time they kick the ball through either of the small goals. Play games for 20 to 30 minutes. The team that scores the most points wins the game.

Coaching Points.

The attackers should combine one- and two-touch passing with player movement away from the ball to create scoring opportunities. The four defenders must position themselves to cover the most critical space, the areas from which goals are most likely to be scored. Emphasize that, because they are outnumbered six to four, defending players should counterattack with caution after gaining possession of the ball. Discourage reckless chances in the defending third of the field where mistakes often result in goals scored against.

GAME 60

Four Zone Passing Game

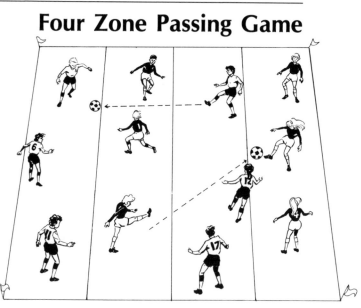

Objectives.

To improve passing accuracy; to develop support movement of players away from the ball.

Equipment.

Cones, flags, shirts, or shoes to mark the playing area. Two balls per game.

Organization.

Organize players into two teams of six; split each team into two groups of three players. Play games on an area 20 by 40 yards sectioned into four consecutive 20 by 10 yard zones numbered 1 through 4. Position three players from Team A in Zone 1 and their three teammates in Zone 3. Station Team B players in Zones 2 and 4. All players must remain in their assigned zone throughout the game. Give each team possession of a ball.

Directions.

At your command the games begin. The objective is for players in one zone to pass their ball *through* the adjoining zone to teammates in the other zone. Players on the opposing team try to intercept passes traveling through their zone. Teammates may interpass within a zone until a gap opens in the adjoining zone through which they can pass the ball. Teams lose possession of their ball if a pass is intercepted or if they kick the ball out of the playing area. Score 1 team point for each pass completed to teammates in another zone. All passes must travel below the waist. Play games for 10 to 15 minutes. The team that scores the most points wins the game.

Coaching Points.

Encourage players to interpass within their zone to create passing lanes between defenders in the adjoining zone. Teammates stationed in a different zone must work to get into position to receive inter-zone passes.

GAME 61

Direct Kick Competition

Objectives.

To develop the ability to score from direct free kicks; to improve general fitness.

Equipment.

Cones, flags, shirts, or shoes to mark the playing area. One regulation size goal and one minigoal 4 yards wide; if portable goals are not available, cones or flags can be used to represent goalposts. One ball per game.

Organization.

Divide players into equal teams of two or three. Station two teams in an area 40 by 50 yards with the regulation size goal on one end line and the minigoal on the other end line. Position a neutral goalkeeper to play in the regulation goal. Give one team possession of the ball to begin the game.

Directions.

At your signal the team with the ball tries to score from a direct free kick spotted 20 yards from the goal. If the shooter scores with the direct kick, his or her team is awarded 1 point and given another free kick attempt. If the shot is saved, the goalkeeper kicks or passes the ball to the defending team. The defending team can score 1 point by kicking the ball through the minigoal located on the opposite end line. The competition continues until a goal is scored or until the ball leaves the playing area. Play is restarted after each score with a direct free kick at the regulation goal from 20 yards away. Teams alternate taking direct free kicks. Play games for 15 to 20 minutes. The team scoring the most points wins the game.

Coaching Points.

Encourage players to develop the ability to swerve shots. You may allow younger players to practice direct kicks from distances of 10 to 15 yards.

GAME 62

Throw-In at Moving Targets

Objectives.

To improve throw-in technique; to improve mobility and agility of players.

Equipment.

Cones, flags, shirts, or shoes to mark the playing area. Two balls per game.

Organization.

Divide players into three equal teams of between three and five players. Play games in an area 40 by 20 yards divided into three zones; the end zones are 20 by 10 yards and the middle zone is 20 by 20 yards. Position one team in each zone. Players in the outer zones are throwers, players in the middle zone are targets. Give one player in each end zone a ball to start the game.

Directions.

At your command the game begins as the throwers attempt to hit moving targets in the middle zone with a ball. Throwers must use the legal throw-in motion. Targets may not catch or deflect thrown balls; they must try to avoid all contact with the ball. Throwers score 1 team point for each target they hit below the waist. Penalty for an illegal throw is the loss of 1 team point. After a successful hit the ball is returned to the player who threw it. Throws that miss targets and travel through the middle zone are collected by players in the opposite end zone who in turn throw to hit the targets. The first team to score 15 points wins the round. Rotate teams after each round with players from an outer zone moving into the middle zone. Play three rounds.

Coaching Points.

Emphasize the correct throw-in motion. All hits must be below the waist. Encourage the targets to use quick changes of speed and direction to avoid being hit by a throw. You may want to use several balls for games with older players.

GAME 63

Shooter Versus Keeper

Objectives.

To develop power and accuracy for shooting; to provide pressure training for goalkeepers; to improve general fitness of field players and goalkeepers.

Equipment.

Cones, flags, shirts, or shoes to mark the playing area. One regulation size goal. One ball for each player.

Organization.

Divide players into equal teams of three to five players. Station teams in single file approximately 35 yards from the goal and position a goalkeeper in goal. If a regulation field is marked, play on one half of the area. Each player has a ball.

Directions.

At your signal the game begins. Players from each team in turn dribble to the top of the penalty area and shoot to score on the neutral goalkeeper. Players must release their shots from a distance of 18 yards or greater; a player may follow up his or her initial shot to score a rebound if the keeper fails to hold the ball. Once the goalkeeper has secured possession of the ball, however, or if a shot misses the goal, the next shooter begins his or her dribble toward goal. Players must alternate left- and right-footed shots. Play games for 15 minutes. The team that scores the most goals wins the competition.

Coaching Points.

Encourage players to dribble at top speed. They should attempt to place their shots low and to the side of the goalkeeper.

GAME 64

Volley Shooting Game

Objectives.

To improve players' ability to score from volley shots; to develop general endurance.

Equipment.

Cones, flags, shirts, or shoes to mark the playing area. Colored scrimmage vests to differentiate teams. Two portable regulation size goals. If goals are not available use flags or cones to represent goalposts. One ball per game.

Organization.

Divide players into equal teams of between four and six players. Position two teams in a 40 by 50 yard area with a goal on each end line. Do not use goalkeepers. Flip a coin to determine possession of the ball.

Directions.

At your command the game begins. Interpassing among teammates is accomplished by throwing and catching the ball. The player with the ball may take only five steps before passing to a teammate. Players can score goals only by volleying a teammate's pass out of the air through the opponent's goal. The defending team gains possession of the ball when (a) a defending player intercepts a pass, (b) the ball goes out of play off an opponent, (c) an opponent scores a goal, (d) an opponent drops the ball to the ground, or (e) an opponent takes too many steps with the ball. Play games for 20 to 25 minutes. The team that scores the most goals wins the game.

Coaching Points.

Encourage players away from the ball to provide support for the teammate in possession. Players should use accurate short range passes rather than long tosses with little chance of completion. Emphasize that players get their knee over the ball when attempting the volley shot to ensure a low trajectory.

GAME 65

Three Line Shuffle

Objectives.

To improve mobility and agility.

Equipment.

Cones, flags, shirts, or shoes to mark the spot for each column of players. No balls are used.

Organization.

Divide an unlimited number of players into three equal teams. Position teams side by side in single file columns facing you. Allow 5 yards distance between the columns numbered 1, 2, and 3.

Directions.

At your command the game begins. You may choose from among three possible commands. If you call out "Number 1!" Columns 1 and 2 change places using a sideways shuffle motion. If you call out "Number 2!" Columns 2 and 3 change places using the sideways shuffle. If you call out "Number 3!" Columns 1 and 3 change places using the sideways shuffle. Issue your commands in random order so players cannot anticipate the direction of movement. Players must remember that after changing positions they assume the number of the column space to which they have moved. Any player who moves in the wrong direction or to the wrong space is eliminated from the game. Play games for 5 minutes. The team with the most players remaining at the end of the exercise wins the game.

Coaching Points.

Place emphasis on quick lateral movement. Advise players not to cross their legs when shuffling sideways. Success at this game depends on mental concentration as well as instant reactions.

Attack or Defend

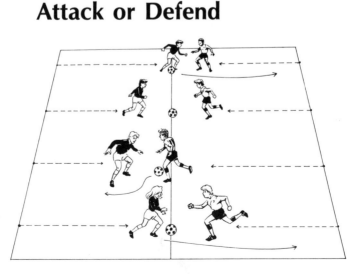

Objectives.

To improve dribbling and tackling skills; to develop individual defending and attacking tactics; to develop general endurance.

Equipment.

Cones, flags, shirts, or shoes to mark the playing area. Colored scrimmage vests to differentiate teams. One ball for every two players.

Organization.

Divide players into two equal teams. Station teams on opposite end lines of an area 40 by 60 yards. Divide the field into two equal halves by marking a midline across the center of the area. Place the soccer balls an equal distance apart along the midline.

Directions.

At your signal the game begins as players from both teams sprint to the midline to secure a ball. Players who gain possession of a ball attempt to dribble it across the opponent's end line; players who do not win a ball try to prevent opponents from dribbling over their end line. One team point is scored for each ball dribbled over the opponent's end line. A player who initially wins possession of a ball but loses it to an opponent before crossing the end line must then defend. The game continues until all soccer balls have been dribbled over an end line or kicked out of the area. The team that totals the most points wins the round. The first team to win 10 rounds wins the game.

Coaching Points.

Encourage dribblers to use feinting movements coupled with change of speed to unbalance and beat their opponents. Defenders should attempt to delay the dribblers and then tackle at an opportune moment.

GAME 67

One-on-One Game

Objectives.

To improve one-on-one marking ability; to develop passing, receiving, and dribbling skills; to develop general endurance.

Equipment.

Cones, flags, shirts, or shoes to mark the playing area. Two portable regulation size goals; if goals are not available use cones or flags to represent goalposts. One ball per game.

Organization.

Divide players into equal teams of five or six. Station teams in a 40 by 50 yard area with a goal positioned on each end line. Do not use goalkeepers.

Directions.

Begin the game with a drop ball at the center of the field. Teams vie for possession of the ball; each team defends one goal and attempts to score in the opponent's goal. Regular soccer rules apply except that the offside law is waived. Goals can be scored from any distance so defending players must use tight man-to-man coverage to prevent their opponents from shooting at the open goal. Each player is responsible for marking a specific opponent. Play games for 20 minutes. The team that scores the most goals wins the game.

Coaching Points.

Instruct defending players to take positions goalside of their opponents in order to block the direct route to goal. Emphasize tight one-on-one marking all over the field.

GAME 68

Join the Hunt

Objectives.

To improve passing skills; to develop agility and mobility; to improve general fitness.

Equipment.

Cones, flags, shirts, or shoes to mark the playing area. One ball for each player.

Organization.

Play with an unlimited number of players. Designate two players with soccer balls as *hunters* and station them outside of the playing area. Station the remaining players without soccer balls in a playing area approximately 30 by 30 yards in size. Place the remaining soccer balls, one for each participant, outside of the area.

Directions.

At your command the two hunters dribble into the area and pass their balls to hit the free players. Passes must strike players below the waist. Free players may move anywhere within the playing area to avoid being hit by a hunter's passes. Players who are hit must get one of the free balls placed outside of the area and join the hunters. Continue the game until all players have been hit with a passed ball and have "joined the hunt." Repeat the game several times choosing different hunters to begin each game.

Coaching Points.

Advise the hunters to dribble near their targets before attempting to pass. You may place restrictions on the game to emphasize a specific type of pass; for example, use inside of the foot only or in-step only. As a variation, require that all passes be made with the players' weaker foot.

GAME 69

Back Door, Front Door

Objectives.

To develop combination passing patterns and player movment away from the ball; to improve one-on-one marking ability; to develop general endurance.

Equipment.

Cones, flags, shirts, or shoes to mark the playing area. One ball per game.

Organization.

Divide players into teams of three. Station two teams in a 30 by 30 yard area; use cones or flags to represent two small goals positioned within the playing area. Do not use goalkeepers.

Directions.

Begin the game with a drop ball at the center of the field. The team that wins possession can score by kicking the ball through either of the two goals; the opposing team must defend both goals. Points can be scored from shots taken on either side of the goals, through either the "back door" or the "front door." When a team loses possession, its players become defenders. A ball that leaves the field area is returned by throw-in. Play games for 15 minutes. The team that scores the most goals wins the game.

Coaching Points.

Emphasize tight one-on-one defensive marking. Stress the importance of immediate transition from attack to defense and vice versa.

GAME 70

Game With Restricted Dribbling

Objectives.

To emphasize the tactical considerations of dribbling in appropriate situations and selected areas of the field; to develop general endurance.

Equipment.

Cones, flags, shirts, or shoes to mark the playing area. Two regulation size goals; if goals are not available use flags or cones to represent goalposts. Colored scrimmage vests to differentiate teams. One ball per game.

Organization.

Divide players into teams of five: four field players and one goalkeeper. Station two teams in an area 60 by 40 yards in size with a goal positioned on each end line. Divide the playing field into three equal zones. Each team defends one goal and tries to score in the other goal. Give one team possession of the ball to start the game.

Directions.

Begin the game with a kickoff from the center of the field. Regular soccer rules are in effect except that certain restrictions apply in the different zones. Players may use only one- and two-touch passing in the defending zone nearest their goal. Players from both teams may use limited dribbling in the middle zone—they are permitted to dribble into open space but may not dribble to take on and beat an opponent. Dribbling is required in the attacking zone of the field nearest the opponent's goal. In that area the player with the ball must beat an opponent by dribbling before passing to a teammate or shooting on goal. Players who violate a zone restriction lose possession of the ball to the opposing team. Play games for 20 minutes. The team that scores the most goals wins the game.

Coaching Points.

From a tactical perspective dribbling should be discouraged in the defending third of the field where one mistake may result in a goal against. Limit excessive dribbling in the middle third because it tends to slow the attack while also increasing the risk of loss of possession. Emphasize that dribbling can be most effective when used in the attacking third of the field in situations where an attacker has been isolated on a single defender.

GAME 71

In and Out

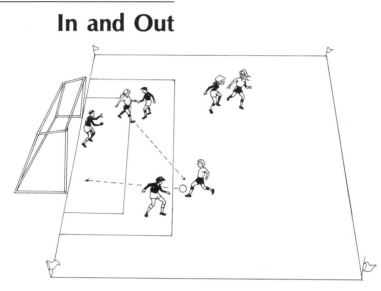

Objectives.
To develop the ability to score after receiving a backpass; to improve general fitness.

Equipment.
Cones, flags, shirts, or shoes to mark the playing area. One regulation size goal; if a goal is not available use flags or cones to represent goalposts. Colored scrimmage vests to differentiate teams. One ball per game.

Organization.
Divide players into teams of three. Station two teams in an area approximately 40 by 50 yards with a regulation goal on one end line. If a regulation field is marked, play on one half of the field. Award one team possession of the ball while the other team defends to start the game. Position a neutral goalkeeper in the goal.

Directions.
At your command the team with the ball begins its attack from approximately the 35-yard line. To score, the attacking team must work the ball into the penalty area before backpassing to a supporting player who can shoot on goal. All shots at goal must originate from a backpass. A goal scored counts 2 points; a shot that is on goal but saved by the keeper counts 1 point. Shots off target count zero points. Except for the method of scoring, regular soccer rules

apply. Teams change possession when (a) the ball goes out of play, (b) a foul or misconduct occurs, (c) a goal is scored, (d) the goalkeeper saves a shot, or (e) a defending player steals the ball. After each change of possession players must return the ball to the 35-yard line before starting the next attack. Play games for 20 to 30 minutes. The team that scores the most points wins the game.

Coaching Points.

The attacking team should use width and depth in its attack to spread out the defending team. Proper support of the player in possession of the ball is required to score from backpasses.

GAME 72

Running Throw-In Game

Objectives.

To improve throw-in technique; to improve general endurance.

Equipment.

Cones, flags, shirts, or shoes to mark the playing area. Two field hockey goals; if goals are not available use flags or cones to represent goalposts. Colored scrimmage vests to differentiate teams. Two balls per game.

Organization.

Divide players into two equal teams of four to seven players. Station teams in an area 30 by 50 yards with a field hockey goal positioned on each end line. Teams defend one goal and try to score in the opponent's goal. Do not use goalkeepers. Give each team possession of a ball.

Directions.

At your command the game begins. Teams can score 1 point each time they throw a ball through the opponent's goal. Interpassing among teammates is accomplished by throwing and catching the ball. Kicking is prohibited. Players must use the correct throw-in motion. Both hands are placed behind the ball and the throwing motion must begin behind the head. Both feet must be touching the ground at the moment the ball is released. Players may take only five steps with a ball before throwing it. Change of possession occurs when (a) a throw is intercepted, (b) the ball goes out of play, (c) a player drops the ball, (d) a goal is scored, or (e) a player makes an improper throw-in. A ball that goes out-of-bounds is returned by throw-in. Although regular goalkeepers are not designated, all players may use their hands to catch the ball or to block shots aimed at their goal. Play games for 20 minutes. The team that scores the most goals wins the game.

Coaching Points.

Emphasize the correct throw-in technique. Players may drag their rear foot along the ground as they throw the ball so long as both feet contact the ground at the moment the ball is released. Emphasize accuracy as well as distance of the throw.

GAME 73

Shooting From Set Pieces

Objectives.

To develop power and accuracy for shooting direct free kicks.

Equipment.

One regulation size goal required per game; if a goal is not available use cones or flags to represent goalposts. One ball for each shooting player.

Organization.

Divide players into groups of three. Two players are shooters and one is in the goal as a neutral goalkeeper. Station the shooters 20 yards in front of the goal.

Directions.

The game begins as the shooters alternate taking direct free kicks at the goal from a distance of 20 to 25 yards. Shooters score 2 points for a goal and 1 point for a shot on goal that is saved by the goalkeeper. Shooters are penalized one point for a shot that travels wide or over the goal. The first player to score 20 points wins the round. Rotate players after each round with the goalkeeper becoming a shooter and one of the original shooters playing as the goalkeeper. Play three rounds.

Coaching Points.

Place emphasis on shooting with power and accuracy. Encourage players to practice swerving their shots by striking the ball with either the inside or outside portion of the instep. For younger players the shooting distance may be reduced to 12 to 15 yards.

GAME 74

Pass and Receive to Score

Objectives.

To improve passing and receiving skills; to improve one-on-one marking ability; to develop endurance.

Equipment.

Cones, flags, shirts, or shoes to mark the playing area. Cones or flags to represent minigoals two yards wide. Colored scrimmage vests to differentiate teams. One ball per game.

Organization.

Divide players into equal teams of four to six. Station two teams in an area 40 by 40 yards; position five small goals within the playing area. Flip a coin to determine possession of the ball.

Directions.

At your command the game begins with a kickoff from the center of the playing area. Teams can score in any of the five goals and must defend all five goals when the opposing team has possession of the ball. Players can score 1 point by kicking the ball through a goal to a teammate on the opposite side of the goal. The shot does not count unless the ball travels along the ground between the goal-posts and a teammate then receives and controls it. Points may be scored from either side of the goals; however, consecutive scores through the same goal are not permitted. A ball out of play is returned by throw-in. Play games for 20 to 30 minutes with no pause in action after a score. The team that scores the most points wins the game.

Coaching Points.

Use one-on-one defensive marking. Encourage players to direct their attack toward the goal area with the fewest defenders.

GAME 75

Tackle All

Objectives.

To improve the block tackle technique; to develop creative dribbling skills; to improve general fitness.

Equipment.

Cones, flags, shirts, or shoes to mark the playing area. One ball for each player, except the defenders.

Organization.

Play with between 10 and 20 players. Designate two players as defenders and position them without balls outside the playing area. Station each player with a ball in a 20 by 20 yard area.

Directions.

The game begins as all players except the two defenders dribble within the playing area. At your command the defenders enter the area and attempt to tackle and win possession of a ball. A player losing possession of the ball becomes a defender and must try to steal someone else's ball. Play games for 10 to 15 minutes.

Coaching Points.

Encourage the defenders to maintain balance and body control at all times. Emphasize the block tackle technique. A player should lock the ankle and use the inside surface of the foot to block the ball away from the dribblers. Discourage use of the slide tackle. You may use three or more defenders to make the game more challenging for the dribblers.

GAME 76

Round the Flag Relay

Objectives.

To improve dribbling speed; to develop general endurance.

Equipment.

Cones, shirts, or shoes to mark the starting line. Flags to mark the turnaround points. One ball per team.

Organization.

Divide players into equal teams of three to five players. Position teams side by side along the starting line in single file columns. Position a flagpost 25 yards in front of each team. Give the first player in each line possession of the ball.

Directions.

At your command the first player in each line dribbles as fast as possible around the flagpost and back to the starting line before exchanging possession of the ball with a teammate. Remaining players in turn dribble the circuit. The team completing the relay in the shortest time is awarded 1 point. Repeat the relay race 10 times. The team that wins the most races is the champion. Each player will have dribbled a distance of approximately 500 yards after 10 races.

Coaching Points.

Remind players that the technique of dribbling into open space differs from that used when dribbling in a crowd of players. To maximize dribbling speed players should push the ball several steps ahead and then stride to catch it.

SECTION II

Games for
Goalkeeper Training

Don't neglect your goalkeeper. He or she is required to perform a set of skills that are markedly different from those used by field players. Techniques for receiving many different types of ground and air balls as well as other important skills must be taught. The following games provide several options that may be used in practice sessions.

GAME 77

Diving to Save

Objectives.

To develop correct diving techniques for goalkeepers.

Equipment.

Cones, flags, shirts, or shoes to mark the playing area. Portable regulation size goals; if goals are not available flags or cones can be used to represent goalposts. One ball per game.

Organization.

Pair goalkeepers A and B for competition. Play games in a 20 by 25 yard area with a goal positioned on each end line. Station goalkeepers on their goal lines and give keeper A possession of a ball.

Directions.

At your command the game begins. Goalkeeper A takes four steps off his or her goal line and attempts to score by volleying or throwing the ball past goalkeeper B. Goalkeeper B may move forward from his or her goal line to narrow the shooting angle. Goalkeeper A is awarded 3 points for a goal scored. Goalkeeper B can score 2 points if he or she saves and holds the shot or 1 point by deflecting the shot wide or over the goal. The shooter is penalized 1 point for a shot off target. After getting possession of the ball goalkeeper B attempts to score on goalkeeper A from the spot where he or she made the save. Keepers alternate taking shots until a goal is scored. After a score both keepers return to their respective goal lines before restarting play. Play games for 15 minutes or a predetermined number of points. The goalkeeper who scores the most points wins the game.

Coaching Points.

Encourage the goalkeeper to move forward from the goal line to narrow the opponent's shooting angle. Emphasize the correct techniques for diving and deflecting shots wide of the goal. Goalkeepers should catch and hold the ball whenever possible to prevent rebounds in the goal area.

GAME 78
___

Saving the Breakaway

Objectives.

To develop the proper technique for saving the breakaway.

Equipment.

Cones, flags, shirts, or shoes to mark the playing area. Portable regulation size goals; if goals are not available flags or cones can be used to represent goalposts. One ball per game.

Organization.

Pair goalkeepers A and B for competition. Play games in a 15 by 20 yard area with a goal positioned on each end line. Station both players on their goal lines and give goalkeeper A possession of the ball.

Directions.

At your command the game begins. Goalkeeper A dribbles forward and tries to score on goalkeeper B either by dribbling past or by passing underneath him or her. Long-range shooting is not permitted; however, rebounds off the goalkeeper from close-in shots are playable. Both goalkeepers return to their respective goal lines after each save or score before starting the next round. Alternate turns attempting to score on a breakaway. Goalkeepers score 1 point for each save. Play games for 15 minutes or a predetermined number of points. The goalkeeper who scores the most points wins the game.

Coaching Points.

Emphasize the proper technique of defending against the breakaway and smothering loose balls in the goal area. The goalkeeper should advance from his or her goal line to confront the dribbling player and reduce the shooting angle.

GAME 79

Penalty Kick Competition

Objectives.

To improve goalkeepers' ability to save penalty kicks; to improve field players' ability to score from penalty kicks.

Equipment.

Cones, flags, shirts, or shoes to mark the playing area. One regulation size goal. One ball per game.

Organization.

Divide players into two teams of six. Five players are shooters and one is a goalkeeper. Mark an 18 by 44 yard penalty area and a penalty kick spot 12 yards in front of the goal; if a regulation field is marked, play in the penalty area and kick from the penalty spot. Place a flagpost 1 yard inside each goalpost on the goal line.

Directions.

Teams alternate shooting penalty kicks against the opposing goalkeeper. Players score 2 points for shots that beat the goalkeeper in the corner of the goal between a goalpost and a flag and 1 point for shots that beat the goalkeeper in the central area of the goal between the flags. Goalkeepers must stand with their feet on the goal line when preparing to save the penalty kick. All other players except the kicker must be outside the penalty area when the kick is taken. Each player attempts 5 penalty kicks for a total of 25 per team. The team that scores the most points wins the game.

Coaching Points.

Emphasize that shots placed in the corners of the goal between a flagpost and goalpost have the greatest chance of beating the goalkeeper. Players should decide where they plan to place their shot well before the kick. Changing one's mind while approaching the ball may hinder concentration and often results in an inaccurate shot. Players must not inadvertently tip off the goalkeeper as to the intended direction of their shot. Encourage the kickers to pick a corner, watch the ball, and shoot with confidence.

GAME 80

Cushion and Catch

Objectives.

To develop goalkeepers' ability to catch the ball; to improve mobility and footwork for goalkeepers.

Equipment.

One ball for each player.

Organization.

Pair goalkeepers for competition. Keepers stand 3 to 4 yards apart and face one another. Each holds a ball in his or her left hand approximately head high.

Directions.

At your command partners begin shuffling sideways in the same direction. While shuffling they simultaneously toss the ball from their left hand to their partner's right hand. Players must receive all tosses with one hand only and are penalized 1 point each time they drop a ball and 1 point for each inaccurate toss. Keepers continue tossing and catching the balls while shuffling back and forth across the width of a playing field. Play games until one keeper is penalized 10 points. Pair players with a different partner and repeat the game.

Coaching Points.

Encourage players to vary the velocity of their tosses. Remind goalkeepers not to cross their legs when they shuffle sideways.

GAME 81

Pingers

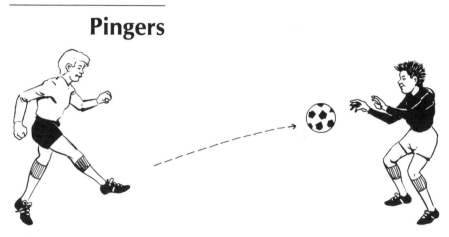

Objectives.

To develop goalkeepers' ability to receive and hold point-blank shots.

Equipment.

Cones, flags, shirts, or shoes to mark the playing area. One ball for two players.

Organization.

Pair goalkeepers for competition. Position players at opposite ends of a 10 by 10 yard area facing one another. Give one keeper possession of the ball.

Directions.

At your command goalkeepers alternate volleying, or pinging, the ball back and forth from a distance of 8 to 10 yards at varying velocities and trajectories. In this game keepers must field all shots with their hands; they may not catch the ball by trapping it against the body. Players are penalized 1 point for each shot they drop. Play games for 15 minutes or a designated number of penalty points. The player who drops the fewest number of shots wins the game.

Coaching Points.

Encourage goalkeepers always to position the body behind the ball as a barrier. Head and hands should be aligned with the oncoming ball. All shots should be received using two hands.

GAME 82

Skippers

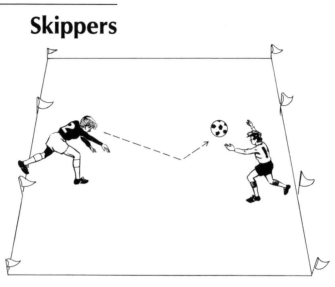

Objectives.

To develop goalkeepers' ability to receive and hold low skipping shots.

Equipment.

Cones, flags, shirts, or shoes to mark the playing area. Two portable regulation size goals; if goals are not available use cones or flags to represent goalposts. One ball for every two players.

Organization.

Pair goalkeepers A and B for competition. Play games in a 15 by 20 yard area with a goal positioned on each end line. Give goalkeeper A possession of the ball. Both keepers take positions on their respective goal lines.

Directions.

At your signal the game begins. Goalkeeper A attempts to score by half-volleying or throwing a skipping shot past goalkeeper B. Keeper A may advance 5 yards off his or her goal line when attempting to score on B. Keeper B may advance only 1 yard off his or her goal line to narrow the shooting angle. A shot that rebounds off B is considered a live ball that A may attempt to finish. Both goalkeepers return to their goal lines after each goal or save and alternate turns attempting to score on one another. A goal scored counts 2 points; players are penalized 1 point if the shot travels wide of the opponent's goal. Play games for 15 minutes or a predetermined number of points. The goalkeeper who scores the most points wins the game.

Coaching Points.

Emphasize the correct technique of fielding the low skipping shot. The goalkeeper should align his or her body with the oncoming ball and dive forward to smother the shot by clutching the ball against the chest. The elbows and arms should be cradled underneath the ball to prevent it from bouncing free. The shot must be handled cleanly to prevent a rebound.

Glossary of Soccer Terms

The following is an abbreviated list of common terms and concepts associated with the sport of soccer.

Agility drills. Exercises designed to improve an individual's range of motion.

Balance in defense. Defensive positioning that provides depth and support. Defenders nearest the ball mark opponents while teammates off-the-ball cover critical space behind the defense.

Ball watching. Defending player focuses concentration solely on the ball and as a result fails to mark the opponent.

Blind-side run. A method of off-the-ball running. Player without the ball runs outside of the opponent's field of vision in order to receive a pass.

Block tackle. Causing an opponent to lose possession by using the inside of the foot to block the ball.

Breakaway. Situation in which an attacker has broken free of all defenders and challenges the goalkeeper one-on-one.

Concentration in defense. Tactic of funneling defenders into the central areas of the field and thus limiting the space available to opposing players in most critical scoring areas.

Counterattack. Team immediately initiates an attack on the opposing goal upon winning possession.

Cover. Defensive support. As a defender challenges an opponent, he or she should be supported from behind by a teammate in the event that the challenging defender is beaten.

Depth. Support positioning both in attack and defense.

Diagonal runs. Designed to penetrate the defense while drawing defenders away from central positions.

Direct free kick. Any free kick that can be scored directly without first touching another player.

Economical training. A training regimen that makes maximal use of practice time.

Endurance training. Prepares players to function at maximum efficiency for the duration of the match.

Far post. The goalpost farthest from the position of the ball.

Flank. Areas of the field that provide a narrow shooting angle on goal.

Full volley. Striking the ball while it is still in the air. The instep is the most common surface used in volleying.

Functional training. Isolating the techniques and tactics of a certain playing position. For example, the skill used by a striker in receiving the ball under pressure of an opponent.

Give-and-go pass. Combination passing in which one player passes to the feet of a moving teammate and then sprints forward to receive a return pass.

Goal side. Defending player positioned between his or her goal and the opponent.

Grids. Confined areas in which soccer skills and tactics are practiced in small groups.

Indirect free kick. A free kick from which a goal cannot be scored directly. The ball must be touched by another player before entering the goal.

Man-to-man defense. Defensive system in which each player is responsible for marking a particular opponent.

Marking. Tight coverage of an opponent.

Mobility. Movement both with and without the ball designed to create space for teammates by drawing opponents into unfavorable positions.

Near post. The goalpost nearest the position of the ball.

Offside rule. A player must have two opponents, including the goalkeeper, between himself or herself and the opposing goal at the moment the ball is played. Otherwise, he or she is offside and is penalized by an indirect free kick awarded to the opposing team. Players cannot be offside if they are positioned in their own half of the field, if the ball was last played by an opponent, or if they received the ball directly from a corner kick, throw-in, goal kick, or drop ball.

One-on-one defense. Defensive system in which each player is responsible for marking a particular opponent.

One-touch passing. Interpassing among teammates without stopping the ball; also called first-time passing.

Overlap. A supporting teammate runs from behind to a position forward of the player with the ball. The overlap is often used as a tactic to move defenders into attacking positions.

Restarts. Methods of initiating play after a stoppage in action. Restarts include direct and indirect free kicks, throw-ins, corner kicks, goal kicks, and the drop ball.

Running off-the-ball. Player movement without the ball that creates passing and scoring opportunities for teammates.

Shielding. Player positions his or her body between the opponent and the ball to maintain possession.

Stamina. Endurance; the ability to perform at a high level of intensity for an extended period.

Support. Movement of players into positions that provide passing options for the teammate in possession of the ball.

Tactics. Organizational concept, on an individual, group, and team basis, of player roles within the team structure.

Techniques. Soccer skills that include passing, receiving, heading, dribbling, shooting, and shielding.

Throw-in. Method of restarting play after the ball has traveled outside the touchlines. The ball must be thrown with two hands directly over the head. Both feet must be in contact with the ground at the moment the ball is released.

Touchline. Side boundary lines of the field.

Two-touch passing. Type of interpassing in which the receiving player controls the ball with his or her first touch and passes to a teammate on the second touch.

Wall pass. Combination passing with one player serving as a wall to redirect the path of the ball. The player in possession passes off the wall and immediately sprints forward into open space to receive the return pass.

Warm-up. Exercises that prepare the body, both physically and mentally, for strenuous training or actual match play.

Width in attack. Tactic of using the width of the field to attempt to draw defending players away from central positions. The objective is to create space for scoring opportunities in the most dangerous attacking zones.

Zonal defense. Defensive system in which each player is responsible for defending a certain area of the field.

Bibliography

Chyzowych, W. (1979). *The official soccer book of the United States Soccer Federation.* New York: Rand McNally.

Henshaw, R. (1979). *The encyclopedia of world soccer.* Washington, DC: New Republic Books.

Hughes, C. (1980). *Soccer tactics and skills.* London: Queen Anne Press.

Lammich, G., & Kadow, H. (1977). *Games for football training.* London: Pelham Books.

Luxbacher, J. (1981). *Soccer: A guide for players, coaches and fans.* Tulsa: Winchester Press.

Luxbacher, J., & Klein, G. (1983). *The soccer goalkeeper: A guide for players and coaches.* New York: Leisure Press.

Luxbacher, J. (1986). *Soccer: Winning techniques.* Dubuque: Eddie Bowers.

Index

About the Author

Joe Luxbacher is a former professional player in the North American Soccer League (NASL), the American Soccer League (ASL), and the Major Indoor Soccer League (MISL). He has coached varsity soccer at two colleges and holds the A Coaching Certificate of the United States Soccer Federation. He serves as a consultant at soccer camps and clinics throughout the eastern United States and is a co-director of Keystone Soccer Kamps. He has published articles on health-fitness, nutrition and weight control, outdoor recreation, and sport psychology-sociology. He holds a PhD in Health, Physical, and Recreation Education and has published three previous books.